THE COLLECTOR'S PRICE GUIDE TO
BOTTLES, TOBACCO TINS, AND RELICS

Here is the best, most accurate and up-to-date introduction you can have to the hottest hobby and collector's craze in America today. In big cities and small, in the suburbs, and out on the farm, people from eight to eighty are collecting, buying, and trading these colorful mementos of America's past.

This volume, fully illustrated in color and black-and-white photographs of hundreds of samples, will tell you all you need to know about starting, building, and maintaining a satisfying and enviable collection.

COLLECTOR'S PRICE GUIDE TO BOTTLES, TOBACCO TINS, AND RELICS

by Marvin and Helen Davis

GALAHAD BOOKS

Acknowledgements

TERRY SKIBBY—*Photography*
DON DAVIS—*Sketches*
VICKI DEDRICK—*Sketches*
L & K ANTIQUES—*Jim Beam Bottles*
RAY SKIBBY—*Insulators*
LOREN D. LOVE—*Tobacco Tins*
JOEY GRAHAM—*Tobacco Tins*
HOWARD HEITZ—*Bottles*
JEWEL BABB—*Bottles*
NELSON'S BOTTLE SHOP—*Bottles*

Published by Galahad Books, a division of
A & W Promotional Book Corp., 95 Madison Avenue,
New York, N. Y. 10016, by arrangement with
Winema Publications, Ashland, Oregon.

Designed by Harold Franklin

Library of Congress Catalog Card No.: 73–54321

ISBN: 0–88365–191–2

Manufactured in the United States of America

Portions of this book were published previously
as *Bottles and Relics, Antique Bottles,* and
Tobacco Tins.

CONTENTS

page

The Bottle Collector / 7
Bottle Collecting / 8
Where and What to Look For / 8
Things to Look For / 10
Tools Needed / 12
How to Clean Bottles / 13
Values / 14
Where to Sell / 14
How to Display / 15

WHISKEY BOTTLES
  intro / 16
  color illustrations / 17 - 22
  black & white illustrations / 54 - 61

JIM BEAMS
  color illustrations / 23 - 31
  intro / 62
  black & white illustrations / 63 - 66
  state series prices / 67 - 69

BITTERS BOTTLES
  color illustrations / 32 - 34
  intro / 70
  black & white illustrations / 71 - 74

MEDICINE AND CONDIMENT BOTTLES
  color illustrations / 35 - 42
  intro / 75
  black & white illustrations / 76 - 89

SODA, MINERAL WATER, BEERS AND ALES
  intro / 43
  color illustrations / 44 - 48
  black & white illustrations / 49 - 53

RELICS
    intro / 90
    black & white illustrations / 91 - 121
    color illustration / 149

INSULATORS
    intro / 122
    black & white illustrations / 123 - 134
    color illustrations / 150 - 153

TREASURE HUNTING
    intro / 135
    black & white illustrations / 136 - 143

FRUIT JARS
    intro / 144
    color illustrations / 145 - 148

TOBACCO TINS
    general intro / 154 - 155
    Store Tins
        intro / 177
        color illustrations / 156 - 157
    Lunch Box Tins
        intro / 178
        color illustrations / 158 - 160
    Round Pail and Canister Tins
        intro / 179
        color illustrations / 161 - 162
    Pocket and Sample Tins
        intro / 180
        color illustrations / 163 - 165
    Miscellaneous Tobacco Tins
        intro / 181
        color illustrations / 166 - 175
    Tobacco Advertising
        intro / 182
        black & white illustrations / 183 - 203

INDEX / 204

THE BOTTLE COLLECTOR

THE BOTTLE COLLECTOR IS a new breed of person. He likes the great outdoors, whether it be the mountains, the desert, or the prairie, he loves being there!

The bottle collector is very much interested in the colorful history of our country and our ancestors. He's a person that can stand in the street of an old ghost town and see it as it was so long ago, with its horse drawn buggies and wagons bustling up and down the dusty streets, the women with their long dresses and colorful bonnets; the men, their bearded faces reddened and rough from years of exposure to the sun and wind and the children yelling and laughing as they run barefoot up the street.

The bottle collector is a person that can look at the remains of our past and see the hidden beauty that lies there. He is a person that wants to be able to take a piece of the past home with him to keep and to cherish. He finds this in the beautiful antique bottles left behind by our past generations.

The true bottle collector can visualize many things about his bottles: The old "whiskey" bottles that used to quench the thirst of the cattle drover after the round up, the miner just returned from making that big strike, or the "city dude" just out for a good time, the "bitters" which was supposed to cure everything from an ingrown toenail to appendicitis, the "pop" bottles which must have made many children's trip to town a happy one.

Most of us are always wanting to find out as much about the history of our bottles as we possibly can. We do this through research that we get from the many books and articles that we find on bottles, and through writing letters to companies and inquiring about a certain bottle. We also find that we can learn much about our bottles by talking to the "oldtimers" themselves, for they actually lived a part of this colorful and unforgettable past. We, the bottle collectors, can relive a part of our colorful pioneer history and share it with others through our bottle collections.

BOTTLE COLLECTING

BOTTLE COLLECTING HAS RECENTLY become one of the most popular hobbies in the country, but was almost unheard of just a few short years ago. It is one of the less expensive hobbies and offers more thrills and excitement than most of the others. There is the thrill and the beauty of the great outdoors; the mountains with their towering evergreens and rippling streams, the lakes with their shimmering beauty, the prairies with their ghost towns and colorful history. There's the wild flowers painting the hills and valleys, the clouds forming beautiful patterns in the turquoise-blue sky, the wildlife roaming the mountains and valleys, the red and gold sunsets, the call of the coyote, the Great Horned Owl and the Meadowlark, the smell of the sagebrush after a thunder shower, and all of the other wondrous beauty of mother nature.

There is the thrill of exploring the old ghost towns, homesteads and mines. The bottle digger can enjoy all this and more. Experience the excitement of digging valuable old bottles from dumps that have been covered over for decades. Thrill to the discovery of rare bitters bottles so highly sought after by collectors, the beautiful whiskies and funny medicine bottles, and the many shades of green, blue, amber and amethyst that tint the bottles. This is just a small part of the reward waiting for the adventurer, the bottle collector, for you!

WHERE AND WHAT TO LOOK FOR

SOME OF THE BEST PLACES to look for old bottles are: old homesteads, mines, ghost towns, railroad camps and possibly right under your own house. If you live in a home that was built over forty years ago there is a good chance that you may be living on a bottle bonanza. Many people used to throw bottles and cans under their houses to dispose of them and quite often houses were built over small trash piles or dumps. My brother has found dozens of very good bitters, whiskies, sodas, etc. under old houses. I also know many other collectors that have made very good finds under old homes and stores. Many of the bottles found under buildings will still have their paper labels intact, which makes them even more valuable. There are thousands of old bottles lying under the old buildings across the country just waiting for you to find. However, be sure that you obtain permission from the owner before looking for bottles beneath any house or building, whether occupied or not.

Whenever you find a dump and are not sure whether it is old enough, some of the things to look for are amethyst colored glass, broken antique glassware, dishes, silverware, etc., and the older type of tin cans. These cans are easy to identify by their hand soldered tops and seams. Unlike the newer tin cans with their machine applied tops that are rolled under the rim around the top of the can, these old tops were laid on and soldered. They also usually have a soldered-over hole in the middle of the lid and are quite crude looking. These older type cans are always a sign of an old dump.

Another good indication is square nails. When digging in an old dump you will quite often find many antiques besides bottles. You will find old silverware, iron toys, firearms, buttons, button hooks, pottery, glassware, dishes and coins. Don't throw any of these things away if they are intact. There are collectors for all of these items and you can sell or trade them. I have made the sad mistake of throwing many of these pieces aside while digging and forgetting about them. A local bottle and antique dealer recently asked me if I had ever dug up any old iron toys. I told her that I had, but they were badly rusted so I just threw them over my shoulder and forgot about them. I thought she was going to hit me with a bottle. She told me that these could be cleaned up and made to look almost like new. She showed me many she had for sale and told me she had cleaned them up and restored them. They looked great and bring a good price. She told me she would buy them from me or trade me bottles for them. So I think I will start back tracking on some of my old diggings and gather up all of those old iron toys and do myself a little horse trading.

While most all collectors prefer to dig their own bottles they also buy and trade for some. So remember all of the other antiques that you find while digging bottles make good trading material.

THINGS TO LOOK FOR

Applied Lip—A good way to distinguish an old bottle is by observing the mold seams. On your older bottles the neck was applied after the bottle was removed from the blow pipe, hence the name applied lip. If the seams end below the top of the lip it is an applied top; if the seams run all the way to the top, the bottle was machine made.

Pontil Marks—A pontil mark is a round jagged scar found on the bottom of many free blow bottles. It was left by the pontil, which was a steel rod that was dipped into the molten glass and applied to the bottom of the bottle, so that it could be removed from the blowpipe. After the lip of the bottle was applied the pontil was removed by giving it a sharp tap, which broke it away from the glass, leaving the round, sharp, jagged scar.

Turn Mold Bottles—A bottle formed in a turn mold will not have seam marks, as a special kind of paste was put into the mold which made it possible to turn the bottle in the mold and erase the seam marks. The finished product was a very lusterous looking bottle without seam marks. Most wine bottles were of the turn mold type.

Whittle Mold Bottles—A bottle that was formed in a mold which was carved out of wood is a real prize, as the whittle marks are left in the glass. In many whittle mold bottles you can even see the grain of the wood imprinted into the glass. Whittle mold bottles are always in very high demand, and bring very good prices. However, not all bottles with a whittle mold appearance were genuine . . . a whittle mold appearance was sometimes caused when the glass was too cool at the time it was placed in the mold.

Sheared Lip—A sheared lip is the sign of an old bottle and is quite rare. After the bottle was formed a pair of clippers was used to clip the hot glass from the blow pipe, "the glass, when hot, cut like leather," this left a sheared neck to which no top was applied, however. Sometimes the sheared top was slightly flanged giving the lip a very slight funnel appearance.

Three Piece Mold—Bottles formed in a three piece mold are fairly rare. This mold came in three sections. The bottom part of the bottle was formed in one piece, and from about the shoulders up the mold was in two pieces. A bottle formed in a three piece mold is quite easy to identify by the mold marks.

Inside Threads—A bottle with threads inside the lip is a desired bottle by most collectors, as they are fairly rare. A special hard rubber stopper was designed to screw into the threads. Most bottles with inside threads are whiskies. These bottles bring a much better price than the ordinary cork type bottle.

Kickup Bottoms—A kickup bottom is one that is indented. Some of them are just slightly indented, while others are deeply indented. Many wine bottles have kickup bottoms.

Round Bottoms—Many soda and mineral water bottles have round bottoms, some of them are actually torpedo shaped. These bottles were made of very thick glass to withstand the pressure of carbonated beverages. They were designed to be laid on their sides in order to keep the cork moist and thus prevent it from shrinking and popping out.

Blob Tops—Most soda and mineral water bottles had blob tops, which was a large blob of thick glass around the lip of the bottle. A wire usually ran over or through the stopper and fastened around the neck of the bottle just below the blob top. This held the stopper in place and prevented the carbonation pressure from escaping.

Blob Seals—Some bottles will have a coin shaped blob of glass applied on the shoulder with the name of the company, product, dates, etc. embossed onto it. Bottles with blob seals on them are very popular.

Opalization—You will find many bottles with a frosty appearance, and even beautiful rainbow colors running through them. This is called opalization and is caused by minerals in the ground that stain the glass. It is almost impossible to remove this stain from a bottle.

Imperfections—Most of your old bottles will have imperfections such as bubbles, crooked necks, dents in the glass, etc. This just makes a bottle more desired by collectors. The more imperfections a bottle has the more valuable it is.

TOOLS NEEDED

THERE IS QUITE A VARIETY of tools used by the bottle digger. Shovel, potato fork, small hand spade, rake, hoe and putty knife are some. The bottle digger should also wear leather gloves as cuts from broken glass or rusty tin cans can be dangerous. Most diggers seem to prefer the potato fork as they are less apt to break a bottle with this tool. I prefer a short handled shovel.

Regardless of what type of tool you use you should dig very carefully. This will lessen chances of breaking any bottles and most bottle diggers know how disheartening it is to break a bottle that you have worked so hard to find, especially a good bitters, whiskey, etc.

When you locate a bottle still partly embedded in dirt it is a good idea to have a small tool to finish digging it out. Some good tools for this are a small hand spade, cement trowel, butter knife or putty knife. With these tools you can loosen the dirt around the bottle without too much danger of breaking it.

Another good thing to have along is a stack of newspapers to wrap the bottles in before placing them in a cardboard box. Old bottles should be handled very carefully as some are quite fragile.

HOW TO CLEAN BOTTLES

WE HAVE RECEIVED MANY LETTERS from people wanting to know how to clean their bottles. There are lots of methods being used, but regardless of what method is used some bottles cannot be completely cleaned. Mineral stains are the hardest to remove and in most cases they cannot be removed at all because they run all the way through the glass. Some of these stains etch the glass beautifully or create beautiful rainbow colors. This is called opalization of the glass. While opalized bottles are preferred by many collectors, I do not care for opalized bottles even though I have seen some that I would like to have had in my collection. You will find many opalized bottles in an old dump that had been burned. Many of the bottles are not damaged by the fire, but after laying in the ashes for years they will become quite opalized. Many bottles found in coastal communities will be opalized. This is is caused by the salt and high mineral content of the soil.

Some of the methods used for cleaning bottles that we've heard of or used ourselves are: steam iron cleaner, water and sand, vinegar and rice, good old soap and water, lye and certain types of acid, the last two not being recommended for anyone inexperienced in the proper use of lye and acids. Not only is it dangerous but I have seen good bottles ruined with acids. If the bottle is very porous or deeply mineral stained, acid will ruin it.

We clean our bottles using soap, cleanser, scouring pads, and various sizes and shapes of brushes. Brushes that I would recommend are: percolator stem brushes, baby bottle brushes, and wire with cotton swabs on the end. Soak your bottle in warm soapy water for a few hours and then scour the outside with a good scouring pad. Then shake cleanser into the bottle and use your brushes and wire swabs. Then rinse in warm water and dry. Be careful not to use very hot water as you might break some of your bottles.

Pipe stem cleaners work well on tiny bottles, especially opium bottles. Incidentally, use extreme care when washing opium bottles as they are very porous and break very easily. I have washed them and laid them down on a towel and had them crack or break in two, for no apparent reason at all. They are very sensitive to temperature changes.

After you return home from that bottle hunt and you work very hard at trying to clean them and find that no matter how hard you try, you just can't get them all clean, don't dispair; just remember, you've got lots of company, as we all have this same problem.

VALUES

PRICING BOTTLES IS VERY DIFFICULT because a certain bottle will be quite scarce in some areas and common in others. Some collectors will pay a substantial price for a bottle that they want to add to their collection. It's just a matter of supply and demand. A rare bottle will most always bring a good price because all collectors would like to have a bottle in their collection that is different from all others.

There are cases where bottles have sold for as high as two thousand dollars, and as time goes on prices will go higher. Some bottles are more popular than others. Historical flasks are probably the most popular, then bitters, whiskies, sodas, poisons, medicines and condiments in that order.

Other contributing factors in pricing bottles are color, crudeness, and imperfections. For example, a bottle with a very crooked neck will bring more than the same bottle with a straight neck. A bottle that is a deep purple or amethyst will bring more than the same bottle if it is just light pink, or clear; hence, should you dig out bottles that are clear or light pink it would be a good idea to place them where they will receive a maximum of sunlight so they can color nicely. This will raise their value. Bottles will not color in a matter of days or weeks. It takes months or even years of exposure to bright sunlight. Some, however, will color sooner than others, and some darker than others, depending on the amount of manganese used in the batch of glass that the bottle was blown from. You will get more money for your bottles from a collector than a dealer, because the dealer has to make his profit, but a dealer will generally buy larger quantities from you. One last word of advice, never sell your bottle without first checking around, and then sell to the highest bidder.

WHERE TO SELL

THERE ARE MANY PEOPLE that dig bottles to sell, but do not care to collect them. Then there are the collectors that sell or trade duplicates only. When we first got interested in digging bottles we only wanted to sell them, but now only sell or trade our duplicates. I can remember selling many bottles that we would like to have in our collection now.

Antique bottles are always in demand, and therefore are easy to sell, especially good bitters and whiskies. Some of the best ways to sell your bottles are by advertising them in magazines and newspapers or by contacting collectors, bottle shops, and antique stores. There are hundreds of dealers across the country that buy and sell bottles. In my opinion, advertising is the best method, especially when you have good bitters, whiskies, or sodas to sell.

If you live in or close to a large city there will be many bottle and antique dealers for you to contact. Bottle shows or flea markets are another good bet. There are several good magazines and papers on the market that give information and dates on the bottle shows and flea markets. These magazines are also a very good source for your advertising as they are read by thousands of bottle dealers and collectors. One thing for sure, digging and cleaning the bottles is the hard part, selling them is easy.

HOW TO DISPLAY

THERE ARE NUMEROUS WAYS in which a person can display his bottles, insulators or relics. Some of the most attractive that we have observed are achieved by using natural and artificial light. If you are displaying bottles or insulators you can place them in windows around a room and enjoy their beautiful colors by the natural daylight coming through the windows behind them. If you want to invest a little money, you can have display cases with lighting systems installed in them, built and mounted on the walls in your den or living room. Then with just the flip of a switch you have a beautiful display day or night. This is the way we have some of our bottles displayed.

If you really want to do it up big you could have display cases with lighting systems, built right into your walls. This would be an excellent way to display bottles or insulators in a den. This would also be a very attractive way to display relics, only with relics you should use overhead lighting, and with bottles the lighting should be behind frosted glass or a fiberglass partition directly behind the bottles. A beautiful place to display old tobacco cans is on a fireplace mantel. This is also a very good place to display Jim Beam bottles. Jim Beams can also be very beautifully displayed in a dining room hutch.

Room dividers with shelves are a very attractive way to display bottles or relics. There are countless ways one can display his bottles. All it usually takes is a small investment, a little time and imagination. Remember, the way in which you display your bottles and relics can add much to your collection.

WHISKEY BOTTLES

PERHAPS NO OTHER BOTTLE has played a more important part in our colorful history than the whiskey bottle. They were scattered across our prairies, deserts and mountains by the Buffalo Hunter, Prospector and Indian Fighter.

The Indian went wild when he drank the whiteman's firewater, he also found that the broken containers made good points for his arrows. The Cowboy used whiskey to disinfect cuts and scratches. The Gunfighter used it to build his nerve. The doctor used it to disinfect and to help kill pain. The lonely man used it to drown his sorrows.

Yes, Whiskey and its containers had many uses. The Whiskey distilleries sprang up all over the west, and as the damand for glass, containers became greater the glass companies swung into high gear. There were whiskey distributors in most all of the larger cities in the west, San Francisco, Sacramento, Portland, etc. Some of the whiskey bottles that are considered quite rare and are not pictured in this book are listed below:

Chesley's Jockey Club Whiskey
Clear or Amethyst—$50-$100

Columbian Kentucky Bourbon
Amber—$50-$100

Gold Dust Kentucky Bourbon
Clear or Amethyst—$50-$100

Old Judge Kentucky Whiskey
Amber—$35-$50

Teakettle Old Bourbon
Amber—$50-$100

Wm. H. Spears Old Pioneer Whiskey
Amber or Clear—$50-$100

There were hundreds of different brands of whiskey and we have only covered a few in this book. The prices that we have quoted in our book are not to be taken as the last word in pricing your bottles, but are the average price range of these bottles in the western states. The prices will vary in different parts of the country. The price of a bottle, like other collectors items, depends on supply and demand.

[In addition to the colorful illustrations that follow, more Whiskey Bottles are shown on pages 54-61.]

J. F. Cutter
$15–$20

Geo. Benz & Sons
$20–$30

Cyrus Noble
$25–$35

Whiskey
$5–$10

Siebe Bros. & Plageman
$15–$20

Paul Jones
$20–$25

Hannis Dist. Co.
$25–$35

Crown Distilleries
$20–$30

Neals Ambrosia
$100–$300

Brandy
$2–$4

Whiskey
$1–$2

Whiskey
$1–$2

Liquor
Beautiful Whittle
Mold & Kickup Bottom
$25–$35

Levaggi Co.
San Francisco
$10–$15

Hall, Luhrs & Co.
Sacramento
$25–$30

The F. Chevalier Co.
Castle Whiskey
San Francisco, Cal.
$25–$30

G.H. Moore Old Bourbon & Rye
Moore, Hunt & Co.
Sole Agents
$30–$50

Jesse Moore & Co.
Louisville, Ky.

The Duffy Malt
Whiskey Co.
Rochester, N.Y.
$10–$20

Geo. Wisseman
Sacramento, Calif.
$15–$25

Hildebrandt
Posner & Co.
S.F., Cal.
$15–$25

W.J. Van
Schuyver & Co.
Portland
$15–$25

Whiskey
Turn Mold
$3–$5

Duffy Malt Holbrook & Co. Brandy Hall, Luhrs Whiskey Levaggi Co. Whiskey
Whiskey (Believed to be $2–$4 & Co. $2–$4 $10–$15 $1–$2
$10–$20 a sauce bottle) $25–$30
$10–$15

[See pages 54-61 for additional Whiskey Bottle illustrations.]

OREGON
$55–$65

NEW JERSEY–Yellow
$60–$65

WEST VIRGINIA
$140–$150

IDAHO
$90–$100

[See pages 62-69 for additional illustrations and introduction to Jim Beams.]

OHIO
$15–$20

KENTUCKY
$15–$20

PENNSYLVANIA
$15–$20

ILLINOIS
$15–$20

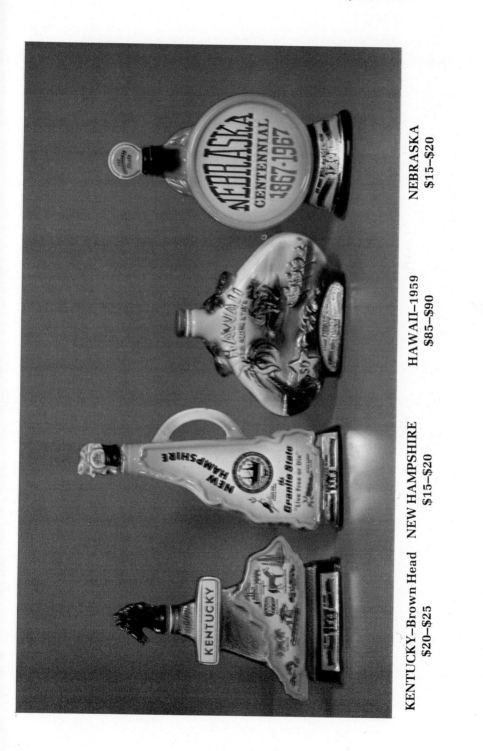

KENTUCKY–Brown Head   NEW HAMPSHIRE   HAWAII–1959   NEBRASKA
     $20–$25 $15–$20 $85–$90 $15–$20

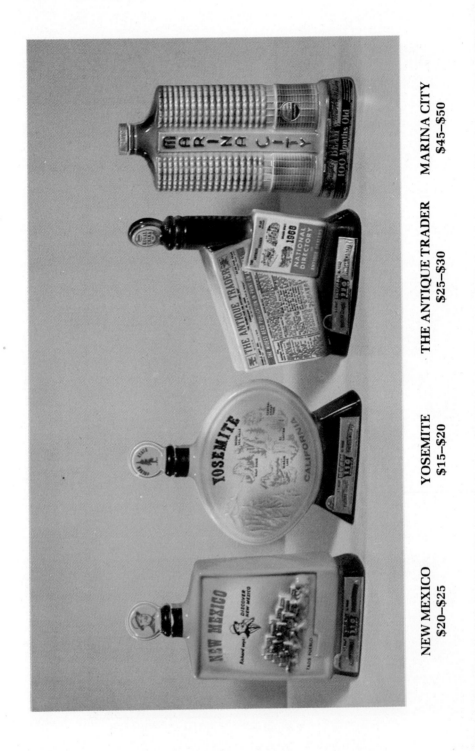

NEW MEXICO   YOSEMITE   THE ANTIQUE TRADER   MARINA CITY
$20–$25 $15–$20 $25–$30 $45–$50

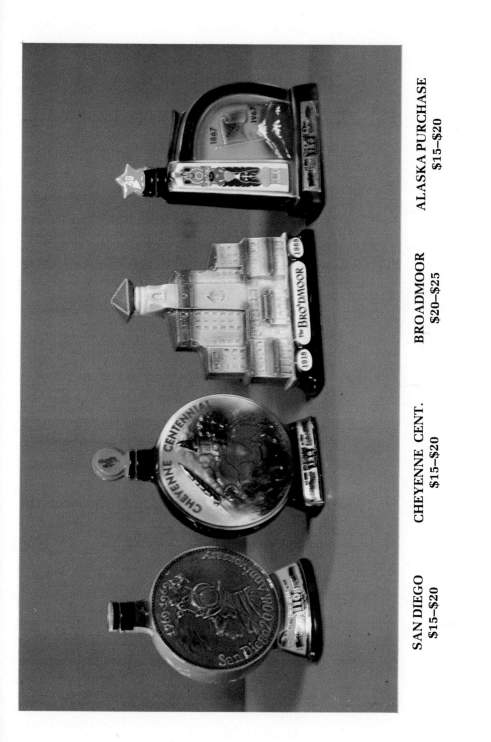

SAN DIEGO
$15–$20

CHEYENNE CENT.
$15–$20

BROADMOOR
$20–$25

ALASKA PURCHASE
$15–$20

ANTIOCH   PONY EXPRESS   REDWOOD   LARAMIE, WYOMING
$15–$20 $20–$25 $15–$20 $15–$20

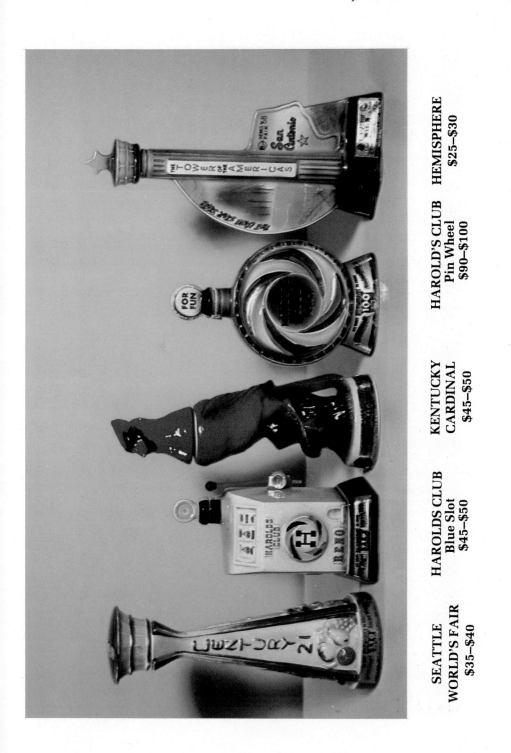

SEATTLE
WORLD'S FAIR
$35–$40

HAROLDS CLUB
Blue Slot
$45–$50

KENTUCKY
CARDINAL
$45–$50

HAROLD'S CLUB
Pin Wheel
$90–$100

HEMISPHERE
$25–$30

BLACK KATZ
$40–$50

FOX
$35–$40

1968 ZIMMERMAN
$15–$20

EAGLE
$15–$20

YELLOW KATZ
$50–$60

1967 PRESTIGE
$25–$30

1966 MAJESTIC
$30–$35

1963 ROYAL ROSE
$55–$60

1965 MARBLED FANTASY
$55–$65

1960 BLUE CHERUB
$90–$100

[See pages 62-69 for additional illustrations and introduction to Jim Beams.]

Dr. Baxter's Mandrake Bitters $10–$12

Caroni Bitters $5–$8

Ernst L. Arp & Kiel Bitters $15–$35

Lash's $10–$15

Dr. J.G.B. Siegert & Hijos $5–$10

Atwood's Jaundice Bitters $12–$15

[See pages 70-74 for additional illustrations and introduction to Bitters Bottles.]

Prickly Ash
Bitters Co.
$35–$45

Lash's Kidney and
Liver Bitters
Oldest Variant
$35–$50

Dr. Henley's
Wild Grape Root
IXL Bitters
$40–$60

Cassin's
Bitters
$100–?

Excelsior
Bitters
$50–$100

Dr. Langley's
Root & Herb
Bitters
$25–$40

Saxlehners
Bitter Quelle
(This is not a bitters, but a
Mineral Water)
$3–$5

Clark's
Sherry
Wine Bitters
$25–$40

Damiana Bitters
Baja, Calif.
$45–$65

[See pages 70-74 for additional illustrations
and introduction to Bitters Bottles.]

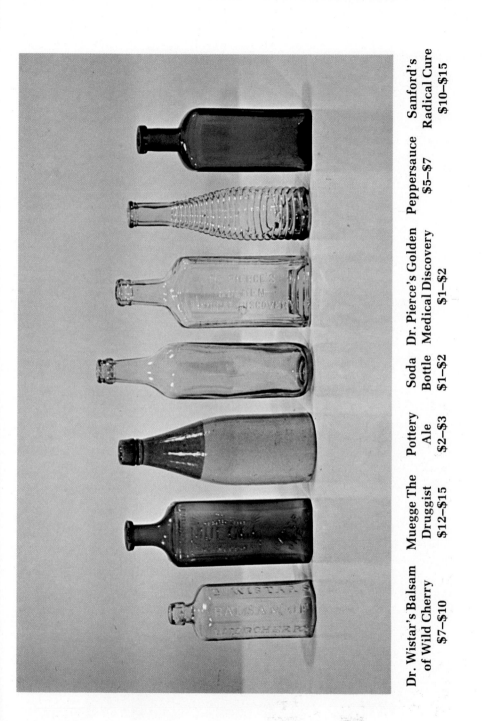

Dr. Wistar's Balsam of Wild Cherry $7–$10

Muegge The Druggist $12–$15

Pottery Ale $2–$3

Soda Bottle $1–$2

Dr. Pierce's Golden Medical Discovery $1–$2

Peppersauce $5–$7

Sanford's Radical Cure $10–$15

[See pages 75-89 for additional illustrations and
introduction to Medicine and Condiment Bottles.]

Lash's Kidney and Liver Bitters $8–$12

Warner's Safe Kidney & Liver Cure Rochester, N.Y. $20–$40

Liquor Turn Mold $1–$3

Dr. J. Hostetter's Stomach Bitters $5–$10

Bottles with labels and contents make a nice addition to any collection and are worth considerably more than the same bottles without labels and contents.

A nice group of poisons. The price range of these would be $1–$2 for the cheapest, $8–$15 for the most expensive. The matched set of four would run $35–$55.

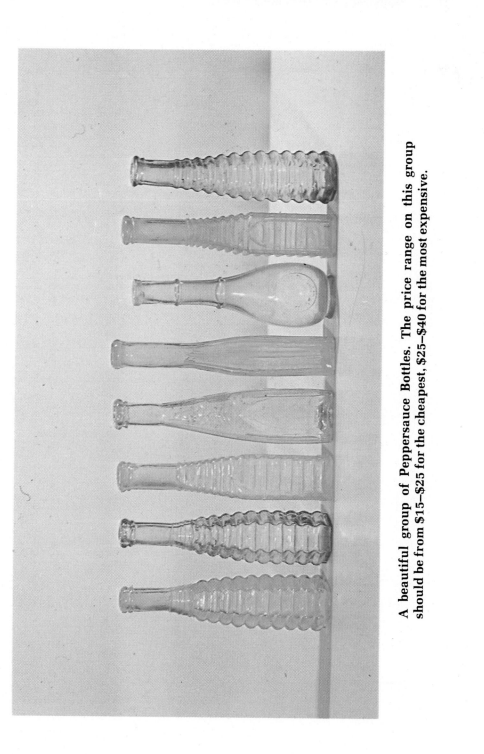

A beautiful group of Peppersauce Bottles. The price range on this group should be from $15–$25 for the cheapest, $25–$40 for the most expensive.

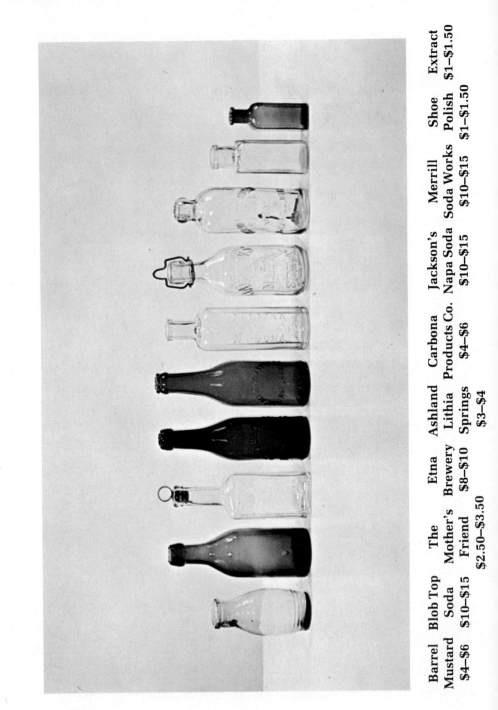

Barrel Mustard $4–$6

Blob Top Soda $10–$15

The Mother's Friend $2.50–$3.50

Etna Brewery $8–$10

Ashland Lithia Springs $3–$4

Carbona Products Co. $4–$6

Jackson's Napa Soda $10–$15

Merrill Soda Works $10–$15

Shoe Polish $1–$1.50

Extract $1–$1.50

H H H Horse
Medicine
DDT 1868
$4–$5

Beverage
Bottle
$3–$5

Prickly Ash
Bitters Co.
$35–$40

Liquor Bottle
Whittle Mold
$25–$30

A van Hoboken
& Co.
$35–$50

Lash's Bitters
Oldest Type
Whittle Mold
$35–$40

Electric
Bitters
$15–$25

Condiment Bottle .50c–$1	Warner's Kidney & Liver Cure $25–$35	Puritana $5–$10	Waw Waw $6–$8	Gde Chartreuse $10–$12	E. Morgan & Sons $3–$5

[See pages 75-89 for additional illustrations and introduction to Medicine and Condiment Bottles.]

SODA, MINERAL WATER, BEERS AND ALES

SODA AND MINERAL WATER bottles became very popular a couple of years ago and then tapered off. Now they are making a strong come back. The blob top sodas are very popular and prices will run anywhere from $8–$25. The cobalt blue sodas are probably the most popular with prices running anywhere from $10—$50. The prices on sodas and mineral waters will vary greatly in different parts of the country. Common type sodas with applied tops will bring from $1—$10.

Coca Cola bottles are very popular, especially the amber colored ones, which are quite rare. Porcelain stopper sodas will bring from $4—$25.

Beer and Ale bottles are also picking up a little in popularity, especially very good embossed specimens. Blob top beers are a good investment.

Eel River Valley Soda Works $7–$15

John Ryan Excelsior Mineral Water $25–$35

J.S.P. $12–$15

Greers Washing Ammonia $5–$10

G. Ebberwein Ginger Ale $15–$25

John Ryan 1866 $25–$35

M.F. & Co. $10–$15

Merrill Soda Works
E.C. Ball Prop.
Merrill, Ore.
$7–$15

Waialua
Soda Works Ltd.
(This bottle is
from Hawaii)
$7–$15

Jackson's
Napa Soda
$7–$15

Simmon's Liver
Regulator
$1–$3

Watkin's
.50c–$1

Eel River Valley   John Ryan   Jackson's   William's Bros.   John Ryan
Soda Works   Excelsior   Napa Soda $12–$16 $15–$25
$10–$15 $15–$25 $10–$15

American Soda   G. W. Angels   Mineral Water   Crystal   Hot Springs
Works $2–$4 $3–$4   Carbonating Co.   Bottling Works
$3–$5 $3–$4 $3–$4

Santa Rosa
Bottling Co.
$10–$15

Whittakers
Altham
$15–$20

Empire Soda
Works
$10–$15

Samuel Soda
Springs
$10–$15

Philipsburg
Bottling Works
$10–$15

G.W. Tallman
Telluride, Colo.
Aqua
$7–$15

Hippler & Brickson
Telluride, Colo.
Aqua
$7–$15

Soda
Whittle Mold
Aqua
$4–$10

Jurgens &
Price Bottlers
Helena, Mont.
Light Green
$7–$15

North Western
Bottling Co.
Butte, Mont.
Aqua
$7–$15

C.O.D. Soda Works Telluride Bottling Co.   Philipsburg   Pioneer Soda Works Fargo Bottling Works Co.
Bakersfield   Telluride, Colo.   Bottling Works   San Francisco   Fargo, N. Dak.
Light Pink   Aqua   Philipsburg, Mont.   Aqua   Light Green
$1–$3 $1–$3 $7–$15 $7–$15 $1–$3

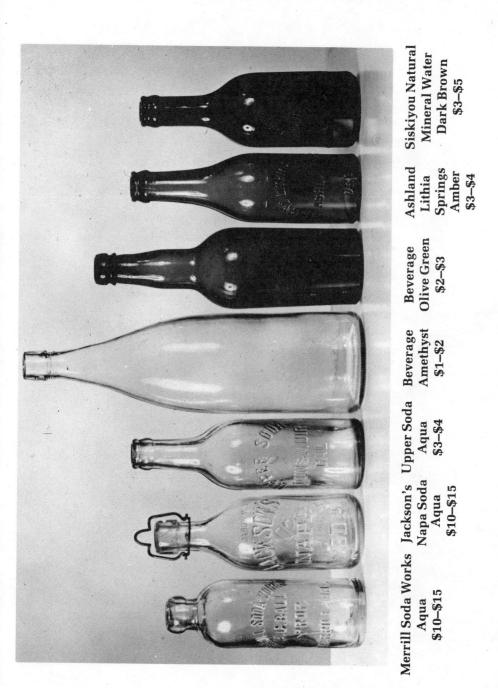

Siskiyou Natural
Mineral Water
Dark Brown
$3–$5

Ashland
Lithia
Springs
Amber
$3–$4

Beverage
Olive Green
$2–$3

Beverage
Amethyst
$1–$2

Upper Soda
Aqua
$3–$4

Jackson's
Napa Soda
Aqua
$10–$15

Merrill Soda Works
Aqua
$10–$15

St. Helena Bottling Co.
Amber
$3–$6

The Stroh
Brewing Co.
Aqua
$3–$5

El Dorado
Brewing Co.
Amber
$4–$7

A. Palmtag & Co.
Amber
$3–$6

California Bottling Co.
Aqua
$3–$6

Lion Brewery Ltd.
Amber
$4–$7

Cambrinus
Bottling Co.
Amber
$4–$7

Claus Wreden
Brewing Co.
Amber
$3–$6

Cal. Bottling Co.
Amber
$3–$6

John Rapp & Son
Amber
$3–$6

Whiskey
Dark Red–Amber
$4–$5

L. T. & Co.
Amber
$15–$20

Whiskey
Amber
$4–$5

Wright & Taylor
Amber
$12–$15

[See pages 16-22 for additional illustrations
and introduction to Whiskey Bottles.]

Louis Taussig & Co.
Clear
$15–$25

Hall, Luhrs & Co.
Clear
$10–$20

J. Rieger & Co.
Light Pink
$15–$20

G.O. Blake's
Clear
$20–$30

Bonnie Bros.
Light Pink
$10–$20

Montebello (wine) Amber $10–$15   Lilienthal & Co. Amber $12–$20   Ciacomini & Boyd Amber $12–$15   Whiskey Amber $5–$10   Oregon Importing Co. Amber $15–$20

Whiskey
Shoofly
Light Amethyst
$1–$2

Whiskey
Amethyst
$1–$2

Whiskey
Amber
$1–$3

Whiskey
Pumpkin Seed or Pic nic
Light Pink
$4–$7

Brandy
Green
$1–$2.50

Whiskey
Amber
$1–$2

Pepper Distillery
Amber
$25–$50

Whiskey
Red-Amber
$2–$4

Gordons Dry Gin
Green
$1–$2

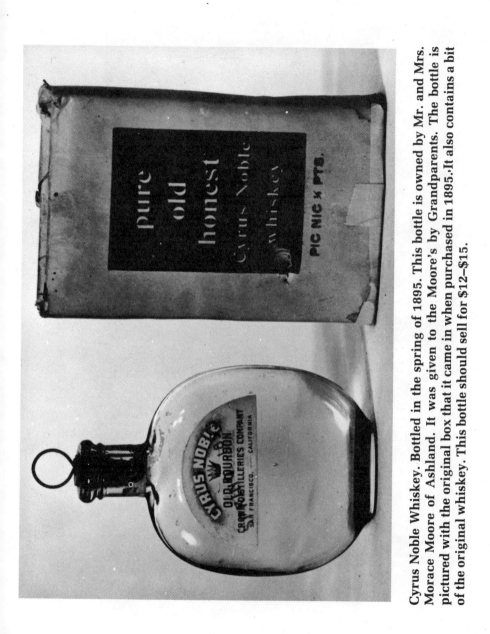

Cyrus Noble Whiskey. Bottled in the spring of 1895. This bottle is owned by Mr. and Mrs. Morace Moore of Ashland. It was given to the Moore's by Grandparents. The bottle is pictured with the original box that it came in when purchased in 1895. It also contains a bit of the original whiskey. This bottle should sell for $12–$15.

W. J. Van Schuyver
& Co.
Amber
$15–$20

Hall, Luhrs & Co.
Amber
$20–$25

H. Varwig & Co.
Amber
$15–$20

Whiskey
Amethyst
$8–$12

L. T. & Co.
Amber
$15–$20

Brown-Forman Co.
Amber
$10–$15

C. H. Moore
Amber
$20–$25

Roth & Co.
Amber
$10–$15

Louis Taussig & Co.
Amethyst
$15–$20

J. H. Cutter
Amber
$10–$15

[See pages 16-22 for additional illustrations
and introduction to Whiskey Bottles.]

JIM BEAMS

No OTHER BOTTLE has gained popularity as rapidly as the beautiful Jim Beams. The Beam Co. began manufacturing their Regal China Bottles in 1955, but the Beam Boom didn't really get under way until about five years ago.

The price on Beam Bottles has skyrocketed and still continues to climb. The First National Bank of Chicago has a price tag of from $2,000-$3,000., and many of the other Beams are going for as much as several hundred dollars each. Some of the Beams that sold for $15-$20 a couple or three years ago are now bringing $100 or more.

A collection of these beautiful bottles is breathtaking to say the least. At this point it looks like collecting Beam Bottles is a sound investment, as well as an interesting and enjoyable hobby. I would suggest that a Beam collection, like any valuable collection be insured, because in a few years it will be almost impossible to replace most of the Beam Bottles, or at least it will cost an awful lot of money. I would also suggest that if you are planning on starting a Beam Collection that you start it as soon as possible, because in a few years these bottles could sell for double what they are selling for now.

The prices quoted in this book will vary somewhat in different areas, but are still a fairly accurate average of the prices being asked for these bottles.

[See pages 23-31 for additional illustrations of Jim Beams.]

ELEPHANT
1964
$15–$20

DONKEY
1964
$15–$20

DONKEY
1968
$12.50–$15

ELEPHANT
1968
$12.50–$15

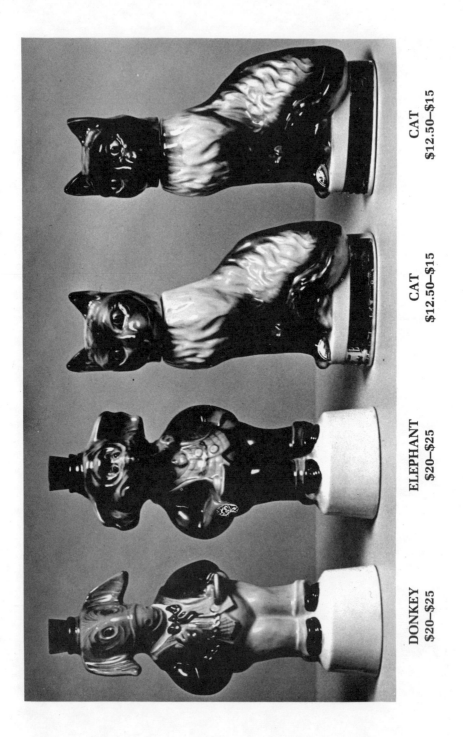

CAT
$12.50–$15

CAT
$12.50–$15

ELEPHANT
$20–$25

DONKEY
$20–$25

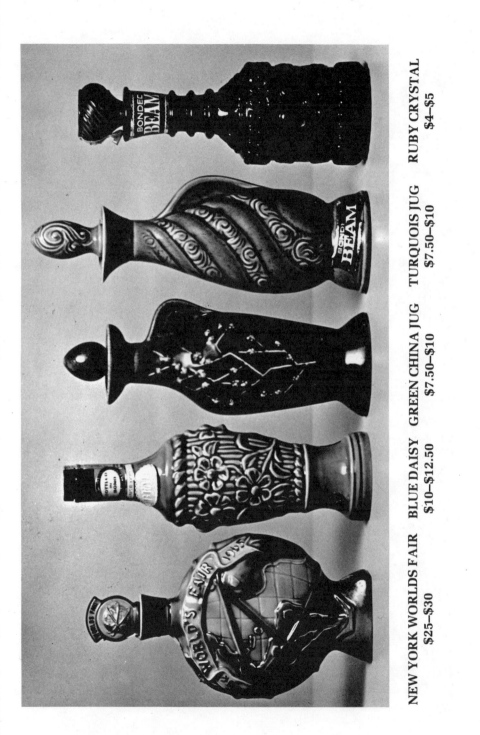

NEW YORK WORLDS FAIR   BLUE DAISY   GREEN CHINA JUG   TURQUOIS JUG   RUBY CRYSTAL
$25–$30 $10–$12.50 $7.50–$10 $7.50–$10 $4–$5

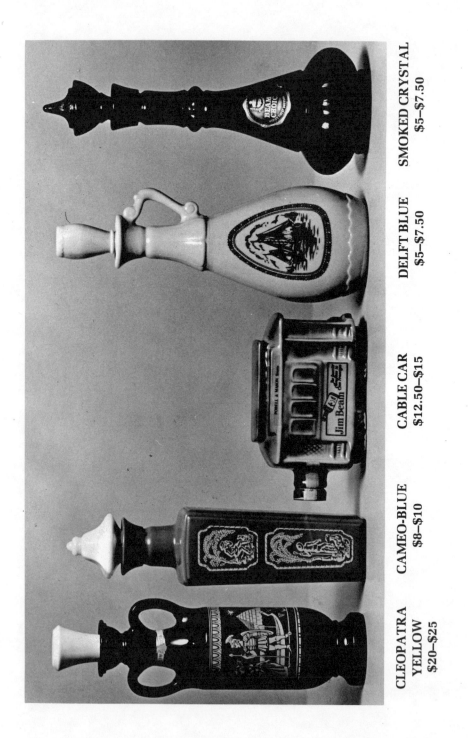

CLEOPATRA YELLOW $20–$25

CAMEO-BLUE $8–$10

CABLE CAR $12.50–$15

DELFT BLUE $5–$7.50

SMOKED CRYSTAL $5–$7.50

STATE SERIES

1958	ALASKA	$ 65—$ 70
1964	& '65 Reissue	$ 50—$ 55
1959	HAWAII	$ 85—$ 90
1967	Reissue	$ 50—$ 55
1959	COLORADO	$ 55—$ 65
1959	OREGON	$ 55—$ 65
1960	KANSAS	$ 70—$ 75
1963	IDAHO	$ 90—$100
1963	WEST VIRGINIA	$140—$150
1963	NEW JERSEY — YELLOW	$ 60—$ 65
1963	NEW JERSEY — GREY	$ 65—$ 70
1963	MONTANA	$100—$110
1963	NEVADA	$ 90—$100
1964	NORTH DAKOTA	$ 80—$ 85
1965	WYOMING	$ 60—$ 65
1966	OHIO	$ 15—$ 20
1967	PENNSYLVANIA	$ 15—$ 20
1967	KENTUCKY — BROWN HEAD	$ 20—$ 25
1967	KENTUCKY — BLACK HEAD	$ 15—$ 20
1967	NEBRASKA	$ 15—$ 20
1967	NEW HAMPSHIRE	$ 15—$ 20
1968	ILLINOIS	$ 15—$ 20

POLITICAL SERIES

1956	ELEPHANT ASH TRAY	$ 20—$ 25
1956	DONKEY ASH TRAY	$ 20—$ 25
1960	ELEPHANT CAMPAIGNER	$ 20—$ 25
1960	DONKEY CAMPAIGNER	$ 20—$ 25
1964	ELEPHANT BOXER	$ 15—$ 20
1964	DONKEY BOXER	$ 15—$ 20
1968	ELEPHANT CLOWN	$12.50—$ 15
1968	DONKEY CLOWN	$12.50—$ 15

CENTENNIAL SERIES

1960	SANTA FE	$175—$200
1961	CIVIL WAR — SOUTH	$ 40—$ 45
1961	CIVIL WAR — NORTH	$ 40—$ 45
1964	ST. LOUIS ARCH	$ 20—$ 25
1966	ALASKA PURCHASE	$ 15—$ 20
1967	CHEYENNE	$ 15—$ 20
1967	ANTIOCH	$ 15—$ 20
1968	SAN DIEGO	$ 15—$ 20
1968	LARAMIE	$ 15—$ 20

EXECUTIVE SERIES

1955	ROYAL PORCELAIN	$165—$175
1956	ROYAL GOLD ROUND	$190—$200
1957	ROYAL DI MONTE	$ 90—$ 95
1958	GREY CHERUB	$120—$130
1959	TAVERN SCENE	$ 85—$ 95

```
1960   BLUE CHERUB ................................................ $ 90—$100
1961   GOLDEN CHALICE ........................................... $ 80—$ 85
1962   FLOWER BASKET ............................................ $ 65—$ 70
1963   ROYAL ROSE ............................................... $ 55—$ 60
1964   ROYAL GOLD DIAMOND ...................................... $ 50—$ 55
1965   MARBLED FANTASY ......................................... $ 55—$ 65
1966   MAJESTIC ................................................. $ 30—$ 35
1967   PRESTIGE ................................................. $ 25—$ 30
1968   EXECUTIVE ................................................ $ 20—$ 25
```

TROPHY SERIES

```
1957   DUCK ..................................................... $ 70—$ 75
1957   FISH ..................................................... $ 70—$ 75
1958   RAM ...................................................... $ 90—$100
1959   DOG ...................................................... $ 90—$ 95
1961   PHEASANT ................................................. $ 20—$ 25
1966   Reissue .................................................. $ 15—$ 20
1962   BROWN HORSE .............................................. $ 20—$ 25
1967   Reissue .................................................. $ 15—$ 20
1962   BLACK HORSE .............................................. $ 20—$ 25
1967   Reissue .................................................. $ 15—$ 20
1962   GREY HORSE ............................................... $ 20—$ 25
1967   Reissue .................................................. $ 15—$ 20
1963   DOE ...................................................... $ 35—$ 40
1965   FOX ...................................................... $ 35—$ 40
1967   Reissue .................................................. $ 15—$ 25
1966   EAGLE .................................................... $ 15—$ 20
1967   TABBY CAT ................................................$12.50—$ 15
1967   SIAMESE CAT ..............................................$12.50—$ 15
1967   BURMESE CAT ..............................................$12.50—$ 15
```

CUSTOMER SPECIALTIES

```
1956   FOREMOST GREY & GOLD ..................................... $110—$125
1956   FOREMOST BLACK & GOLD .................................... $110—$125
1956   PINK SPECKLED ............................................ $240—$250
1957   HAROLDS CLUB SILVER ...................................... $ 45—$ 50
1957   HAROLDS MAN IN BARREL — 1 ................................ $350—$400
1958   HAROLDS MAN IN BARREL — 2 ................................ $275—$325
1962   MARINA CITY .............................................. $ 45—$ 50
1963   HAROLDS CLUB—NEV. — GREY ................................. $150—$175
1963   HARRAHS CLUB—NEV. — GREY ................................. $350—$400
1963   HARRAHS CLUB—NEV. — SILVER ............................... $400—$450
1964   HAROLDS CLUB—NEV. — SILVER ............................... $225—$250
1964   FIRST NATIONAL BANK ...................................$1,800—$2,200
1965   HAROLDS CLUB—PINWHEEL .................................... $ 90—$100
1965   ZIMMERMAN ................................................ $ 85—$ 90
1967   YELLOW KATZ .............................................. $ 50—$ 60
1967   HAROLDS CLUB BLUE SLOT ................................... $ 20—$ 25
1967   HAROLDS CLUB V.I.P. ...................................... $200—$250
1967   RICHARDS NEW MEXICO ...................................... $ 20—$ 25
1968   BROADMOOR HOTEL .......................................... $ 20—$ 25
1968   BLACK KATZ ............................................... $ 40—$ 50
```

REGAL CHINA SPECIALTIES

1955	ASH TRAY	$ 45—$ 50
1962	SEATTLE WORLDS FAIR	$ 35—$ 40
1964	NEW YORK WORLDS FAIR	$ 25—$ 30
1964	MUSICIANS ON WINE CASK	$ 15—$ 20
1965	GREEN CHINA JUG	$7.50—$ 10
1966	TURQUOISE CHINA JUG	$7.50—$ 10
1966	OATMEAL CHINA JUG	$ 50—$ 55
1967	REDWOOD	$ 15—$ 20
1967	YOSEMITE	$ 15—$ 20
1967	ZIMMERMAN BLUE DAISY	$ 15—$ 20
1967	BLUE DAISY	$ 10—$12.50
1967	ANNIVERSARY FOX	$ 45—$ 50
1968	GREY SLOT MACHINE	$12.50—$ 15
1968	CABLE CAR	$12.50—$ 15
1968	KENTUCKY CARDINAL	$ 45—$ 50
1968	PONY EXPRESS	$ 20—$ 25
1968	ANTIQUE TRADER	$ 25—$ 30
1968	RUIDOSO DOWNS	$ 25—$ 30
1968	HEMISPHERE	$ 25—$ 30
1968	ZIMMERMAN	$ 15—$ 20

GLASS SPECIALTIES

1953	COCKTAIL SHAKER	$10.00—$15.00
1953	ROYAL RESERVE	$15.00—$20.00
1954	PYREX COFFEE WARMER	$ 5.00—$ 7.50
1955	DUCKS & GEESE	$20.00—$25.00
1956	PYREX COFFEE WARMER	$ 2.50—$ 4.00
1957	ROYAL OPAL	$15.00—$20.00
1958	ROYAL EMPEROR	$10.00—$15.00
1959	ROYAL CRYSTAL	$12.00—$15.00
1960	OLYMPIAN	$ 5.00—$ 7.50
1961	GRECIAN	$ 5.00—$ 7.50
1962	CLEOPATRA – YELLOW	$20.00—$25.00
1962	CLEOPATRA – RUST	$ 7.50—$10.00
1962	MARK ANTONY	$20.00—$25.00
1963	DELFT BLUE	$ 5.00—$ 7.50
1963	DELFT ROSE	$15.00—$20.00
1963	DANCING SCOT–Short	$30.00—$35.00
1963	DANCING SCOT–Tall	$30.00—$35.00
1964	GENI	$ 5.00—$ 7.50
1965	CAMEO BLUE	$ 8.00—$10.00
1966	PRESSED CRYSTAL SCOTCH	$20.00—$25.00

1966 COLLECTORS EDITION No. 1

LAUGHING CAVALIER	$ 4.00—$ 5.00
ARISTIDE BEFORE EASEL	$ 4.00—$ 5.00
ARISTIDE BRUANT	$ 4.00—$ 5.00
MARDI GRAS	$10.00—$12.00
BLUE BOY	$10.00—$12.00

	ON THE TERRACE	$10.00—$12.00
1967	RUBY CRYSTAL	$ 4.00—$ 5.00
1967	PRESSED CRYSTAL BOURBON	$ 4.00—$ 5.00

1967 COLLECTORS EDITION No. II

NIGHT WATCH	$ 4.00—$ 5.00
PETER SCHOUT	$ 4.00—$ 5.00
GEORGE GISZE	$ 4.00—$ 5.00
NURSE & CHILD	$ 4.00—$ 5.00
SOLDIER & GIRL	$ 4.00—$ 5.00
THE JESTER	$ 4.00—$ 5.00

1968	EMERALD PRESSED CRYSTAL	$ 4.00—$ 5.00

1968 COLLECTORS EDITION No. III

AMERICAN GOTHIC	$ 4.00—$ 5.00
HAULING IN THE GILL NET	$ 4.00—$ 5.00
INDIAN MAIDEN	$ 4.00—$ 5.00
THE SCOUT	$ 4.00—$ 5.00
THE KENTUCKIAN	$ 4.00—$ 5.00
BUFFALO HUNT	$ 4.00—$ 5.00
ON THE TRAIL	$ 4.00—$ 5.00
THE WHISTLERS MOTHER	$ 4.00—$ 5.00
1949-1968 PIN BOTTLES	$ 3.00—$ 4.00
SHORT PIN BOTTLES	$12.00—$15.00

[See pages 23-31 for additional illustrations of Jim Beams.]

BITTERS BOTTLES

BITTERS BOTTLES ARE ONE of the most popular, and are an asset to any bottle collection. There were hundreds of different kinds of bitters manufactured from around the mid 1800's to the 1930's, but due to the ever increasing popularity of these bottles, they are becoming quite hard to find, thus the price of good bitters bottles is fairly high.

Bitters were supposed to cure or relieve anything from bad digestion to headache. I am quite sure that if you drank enough, even though it might not have cured you, you wouldn't have felt any pain, as bitters had a very high alcoholic content. Many people that cursed whiskey and the many other liquors on the market, and swore they would die before they would take a drink of that evil devil's brew, were firm believers in the marvelous powers of these wonderful bitters. They loved the way the bitters relaxed them and made them feel so good again.

Many of the manufacturers of bitters packaged their product in attractive containers to make them more enticing. Some of these containers were shaped like animals, fruits, vegetables and people. These bottles, if you're lucky enough to dig one or can afford to buy one, make an extremely nice addition to a collection. Bitters bottles were manufactured in many colors. Amber, aqua, green and clear were the most common, and these colors can run in many different shades.

Bitters played a very important part in our colorful past and therefore no general collection of antique bottles is complete without a few bitters bottles.

[See pages 32-34 for additional illustrations of Bitters Bottles.]

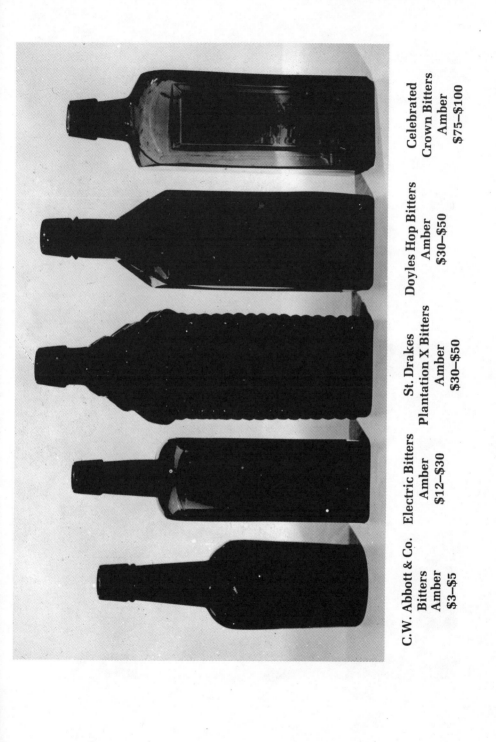

C.W. Abbott & Co.   Electric Bitters   St. Drakes   Doyles Hop Bitters   Celebrated
Bitters   Amber   Plantation X Bitters   Amber   Crown Bitters
Amber $12–$30   Amber $30–$50   Amber
$3–$5 $30–$50 $75–$100

Roehling &
Shultz
Amber
$40–$60

J.A. Gilka
Red-Amber
(Not Bitters)
$10–$20

Bitters
(Ladies Leg)
Green
$25–$35

Dr. Harters
Wild Cherry Bitters
Amber
$25–$35

Peruvian Bitters
Amber
$25—$35

Lash's Bitters
Amber
$8–$12

Dr. J. Hostetter's
Stomach Bitters
Amber
$5–$10

Lash's Bitters
Oldest Variant
Amber
$35–$50

Excelsior Bitters
Amber
$50–$100

Prickly Ash
Bitters Co.
Amber
$30–$45

Electric Bitters
Amber
$12–$30

Duffy Malt
Whiskey
Amber
$10–$20

Geo. Wisseman
Amber
$15 –$25

Levaggi Co.
Amber
$10–$15

Liquor Bottle
Amethyst
$25–$35

Lash's Bitters
Amber
Oldest Type
$35–$50

[See pages 32-34 for additional illustrations of Bitters Bottles.]

MEDICINE AND CONDIMENT BOTTLES

MEDICINE BOTTLES ARE the most heavily collected bottle. This is mainly because there are so many of them. Most people that are just getting started in this hobby quickly acquire quite a collection of medicine bottles because most all dumps have an abundant supply of these bottles.

Although medicine and condiment bottles usually bring less than most of the other bottles, they are still a very desirable bottle due to their many shapes, colors and comical names and claims. Medicine bottle prices will vary from .25c to $50 for the rare ones.

[See pages 35-42 for additional illustrations of Medicine and Condiment Bottles.]

Acid Bottle Lt. Green $1–$2

Durkee's Challence Sauce Aqua $1–$1.50

Sanford's Radical Cure Cobalt Blue $10–$15

Carbona Aqua $3–$5

Johnston's Fluid Beef Deep Wine Red $12–$15

Lea & Perrins Worcestershire Sauce Aqua $1–$1.50

Olive Sauce Bottle Clear $4–$7

Cone Ink Aqua $4–$5

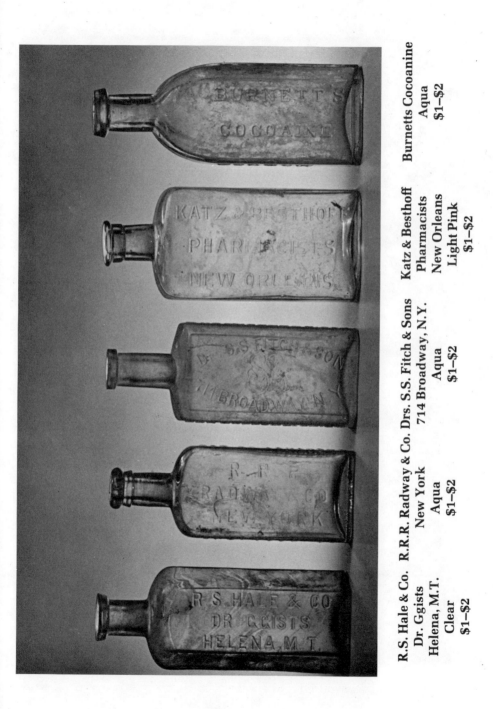

R.S. Hale & Co.
Dr. Ggists
Helena, M.T.
Clear
$1–$2

R.R.R. Radway & Co.
New York
Aqua
$1–$2

Drs. S.S. Fitch & Sons
714 Broadway, N.Y.
Aqua
$1–$2

Katz & Besthoff
Pharmacists
New Orleans
Light Pink
$1–$2

Burnetts Cocoanine
Aqua
$1–$2

Schiedam Voldner's
Aromatic Schnapps
Green
$25–$35

Case Gin
Green
$10–$15

Homer's California
Ginger Brandy
Amber
$7–$10

Johnson Liverpool
Mineral Water
Olive Green
$7–$10

Witter Springs Water
Mineral Water
Amber
$2–$4

A. Trask's
Magnetic
Ointment
Aqua
$1–$2

Medicine
Amber
.25c–.75c

Wakelee's
Camelline
Cobalt Blue
$3–$7

Ayer's Hair Vigor
Cobalt Blue
$3–$7

Laxol
Cobalt Blue
$4–$8

Ink Bottle
Cobalt Blue
$3–$5

Dr. J.H. McLean
Amber
$1–$2

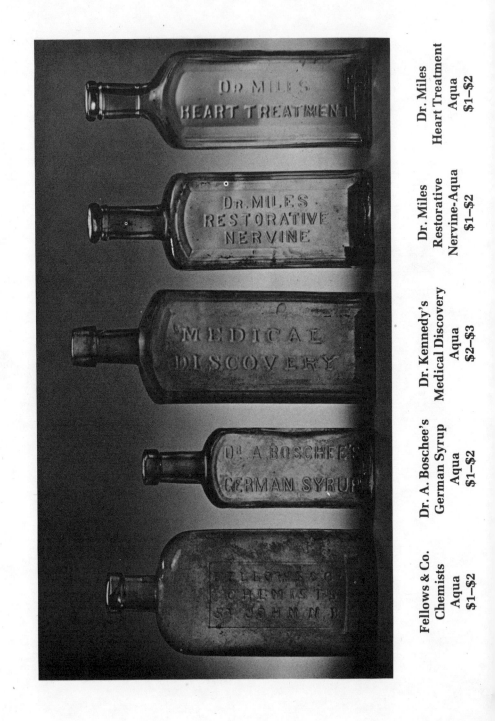

Fellows & Co.
Chemists
Aqua
$1–$2

Dr. A. Boschee's
German Syrup
Aqua
$1–$2

Dr. Kennedy's
Medical Discovery
Aqua
$2–$3

Dr. Miles
Restorative
Nervine-Aqua
$1–$2

Dr. Miles
Heart Treatment
Aqua
$1–$2

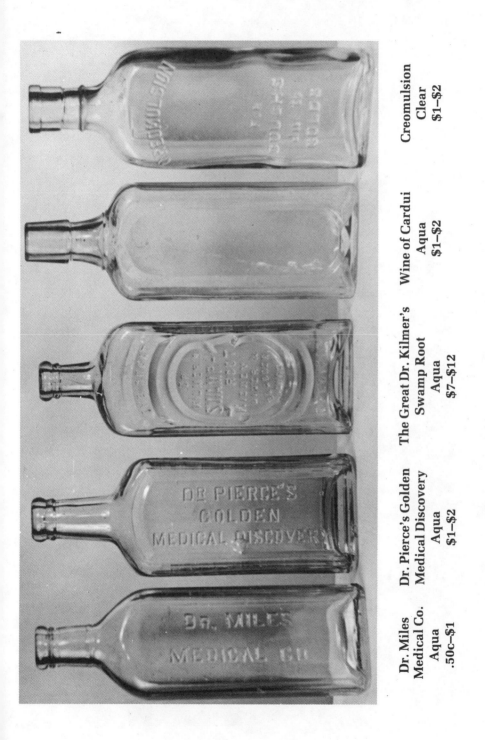

Creomulsion
Clear
$1–$2

Wine of Cardui
Aqua
$1–$2

The Great Dr. Kilmer's
Swamp Root
Aqua
$7–$12

Dr. Pierce's Golden
Medical Discovery
Aqua
$1–$2

Dr. Miles
Medical Co.
Aqua
.50c–$1

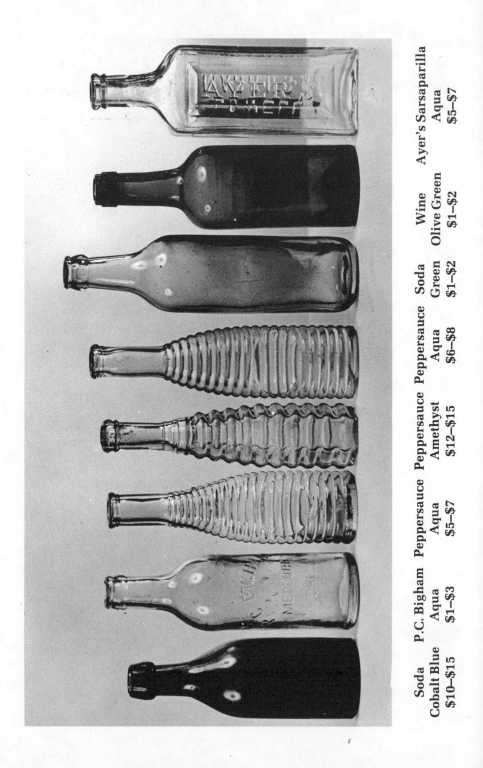

Soda
Cobalt Blue
$10–$15

P.C. Bigham
Aqua
$1–$3

Peppersauce
Aqua
$5–$7

Peppersauce
Amethyst
$12–$15

Peppersauce
Aqua
$6–$8

Soda
Green
$1–$2

Wine
Olive Green
$1–$2

Ayer's Sarsaparilla
Aqua
$5–$7

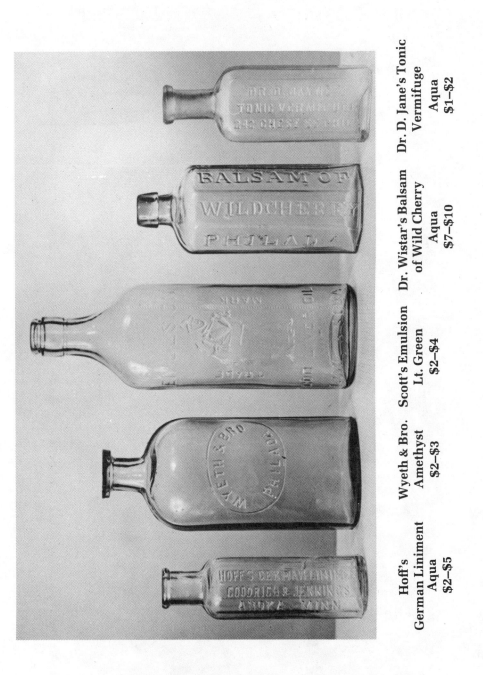

Hoff's
German Liniment
Aqua
$2–$5

Wyeth & Bro.
Amethyst
$2–$3

Scott's Emulsion
Lt. Green
$2–$4

Dr. Wistar's Balsam
of Wild Cherry
Aqua
$7–$10

Dr. D. Jane's Tonic
Vermifuge
Aqua
$1–$2

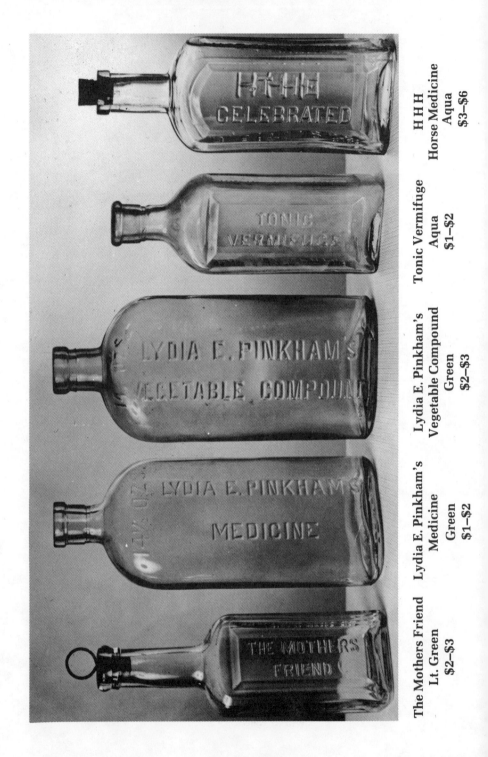

The Mothers Friend
Lt. Green
$2–$3

Lydia E. Pinkham's
Medicine
Green
$1–$2

Lydia E. Pinkham's
Vegetable Compound
Green
$2–$3

Tonic Vermifuge
Aqua
$1–$2

H H H
Horse Medicine
Aqua
$3–$6

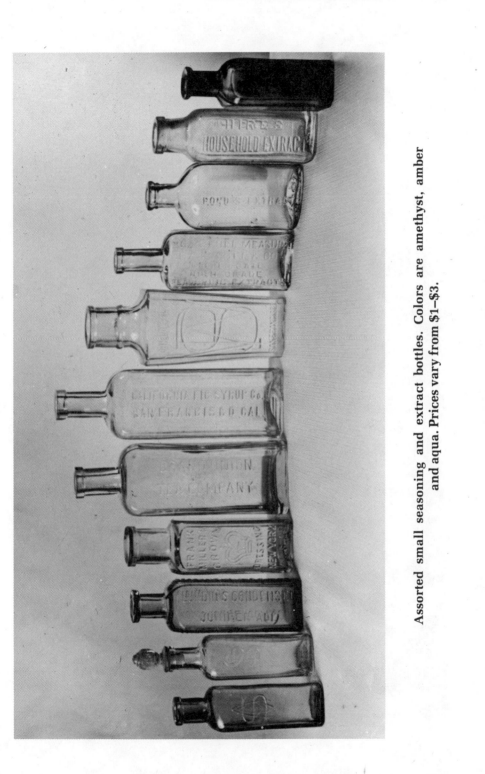

Assorted small seasoning and extract bottles. Colors are amethyst, amber and aqua. Prices vary from $1–$3.

Davis Vegetable Painkiller
Aqua
$1–$2

Whittemore
Aqua
$1–$2

Liquozone
Brown
$1–$2

Hall's Catarrh Cure
Aqua
$1–$2

Chamberlain's Colic, Cholera
& Diarrhea Remedy
Aqua
$1–$2

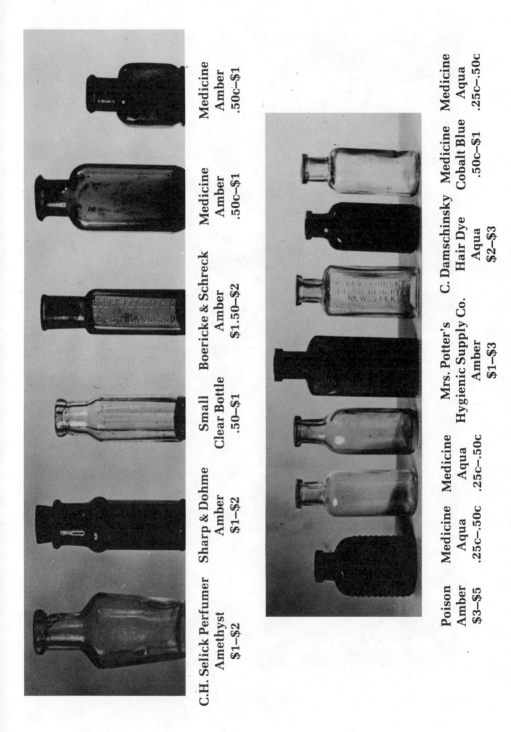

C.H. Selick Perfumer
Amethyst
$1–$2

Sharp & Dohme
Amber
$1–$2

Small
Clear Bottle
.50c–$1

Boericke & Schreck
Amber
$1.50–$2

Medicine
Amber
.50c–$1

Medicine
Amber
.50c–$1

Poison
Amber
$3–$5

Medicine
Aqua
.25c–.50c

Medicine
Aqua
.25c–.50c

Mrs. Potter's
Hygienic Supply Co.
Amber
$1–$3

C. Damschinsky
Hair Dye
Aqua
$2–$3

Medicine
Cobalt Blue
.50c–$1

Medicine
Aqua
.25c–.50c

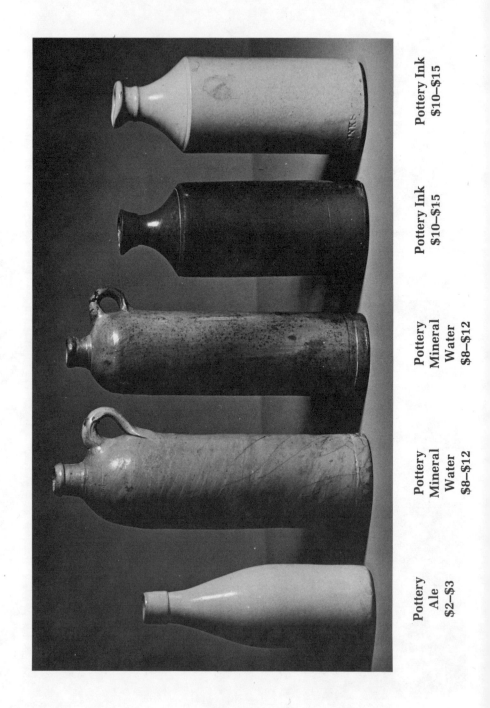

Pottery Ale
$2–$3

Pottery
Mineral
Water
$8–$12

Pottery
Mineral
Water
$8–$12

Pottery Ink
$10–$15

Pottery Ink
$10–$15

CHINESE JUGS—The price on good, undamaged, pieces should be $8–$10 for each of the first three, and $10–$15 for the one with the spout.

[See pages 35-42 for additional illustrations of Medicine and Condiment Bottles.]

RELICS

RELICS, LIKE BOTTLES, are becoming very popular. I predict that relic prices are going to sky rocket within the next few years. Some of the relics that would be a good investment are guns, swords & knives, powder horns & flasks, trivets, andirons, keys, lanterns & lamps, cans, tools, cooking utensils, flat irons & sad irons, canteens, locks, etc.

Prices on relics can range anywhere from less than a dollar to several thousand dollars. The modern day treasure hunter is unearthing many valuable relics with the use of metal detectors. There are also many relics being found in the attics and underneath the old homes and buildings across the country.

We recently received a letter from a young boy who had found an old rifle in extremely fine condition while looking for bottles beneath an old house. He also found several other valuable relics. One of our local business men found a beautiful brass powder flask in an old wood box. There's lots of valuable relics still laying around just waiting to be found, so why not get started in this fun and profitable hobby.

Prices on relics like bottles will vary somewhat in different parts of the country. Many relics that are damaged can easily be repaired. Another very popular type of relic is old toys, these bring a very good price. Relic and bottle collecting go very well together because both are found in the same type of location.

[See page 149 for colorful illustration of Relics.]

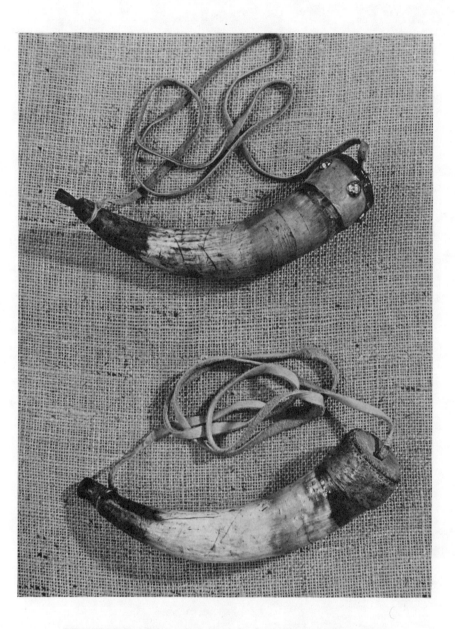

POWDER HORNS—Price of the lower one is $5–$10.
The upper one is $10–$15.

A very nice group of Colts. Upper left—Colt 3rd Model Dragoon—Late 1850's 44 Cal.—$500.—?. Middle Left 1860 Army 44 Cal.—$125—$150. Lower left—1849 Pocket Model 32 Cal.—5 Shot $125 Upper Right—1860 Army 44 Cal.—$200. Middle Right—1851 Navy 36 Cal. $150. Lower Right—1849 Model 31 Cal.—6 Shot $125.

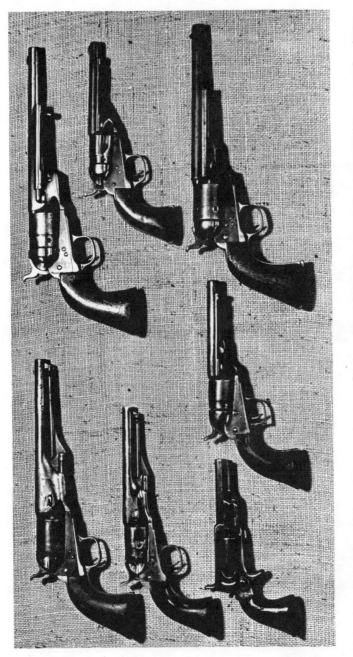

Upper Left 1861 Round Barrel Navy 36 Cal.—$150. Middle Left—1862 New Model Police 36 Cal.—$200. Lower Left—1855 28 Cal.—$150. Lower middle 1853 Converted to 38 Rimfire—$120. Upper Right—1860 Army Converted 44 Rimfire Cartridge—$150. Middle Right—1862 Police Converted to 38 Rimfire—$150. Lower Right 1872 44 Rimfire—$120.

Upper Left—Colt Model 1873 45 Cal. U.S. Army Issue—$200. Lower Left—Colt Model 1873 44-40 Cal Nickel Plate—Ivory Grips—$110-$120. Upper Middle—4 Shot Clover Leaf 41 Rimfire—Silver-plate—$165. Lower Middle 38 Cal. Rimfire Cop & Thug 1870-'75. Upper Right 4 Shot Clover Leaf 41 Rimfire—Earliest model—$165. Middle Right Colt House Pistol 41 Rimfire—$125. Lower Right—5 Shot House Pistol—Silver Plate—$125.

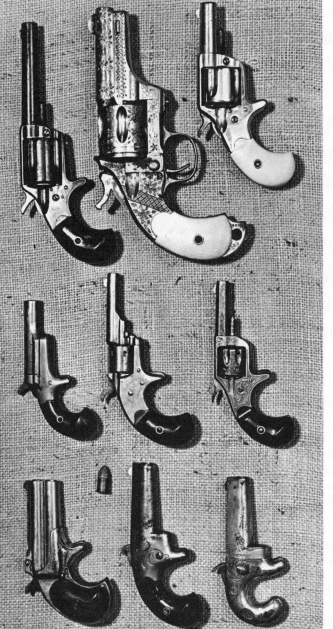

Upper Left—Remington Over & Under 41 Rimfire—$50. Middle Left—Colt No. 2 Derringer 41 Rimfire—$150. Lower Left—Colt No. 1 Derringer 41 Rimfire—$150. Upper Middle—Colt No. 3 Derringer 41 Rimfire—$85. Middle—22 Old Line—$40. Lower Middle—22 New Line, Engraved—$50. Upper Right—New Line 38 Centerfire—$160. Middle Right—Merwin Hulbert 44-40—$150. Lower Right—New Line 41 Centerfire—$50.

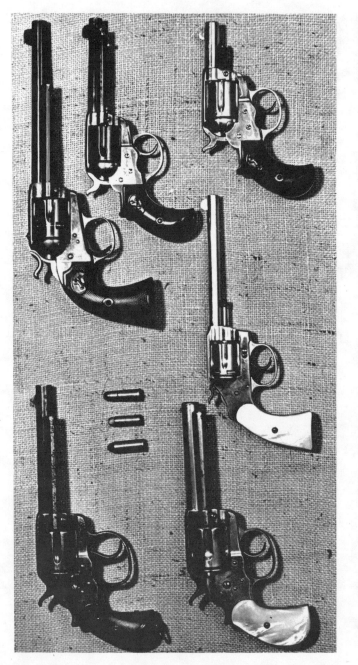

Upper Left—Alaskan model 1902 Army issue Colt 45—$60. Lower Left—Model 1878 45 Colt—$60. Middle—32 Cal. New Police Model. Presentation Nickel—$90. Upper Right—Bisley Model 38 W.C.F. Cal.—$125. Middle Right—Colt Lightening 41 Cal. Center fire—$45. Lower Right—Lightening Storekeeper 38 Cal.—$60. Cartridges pictured left to right—45 Long Colt—41 Long—38-40 W.C.F.

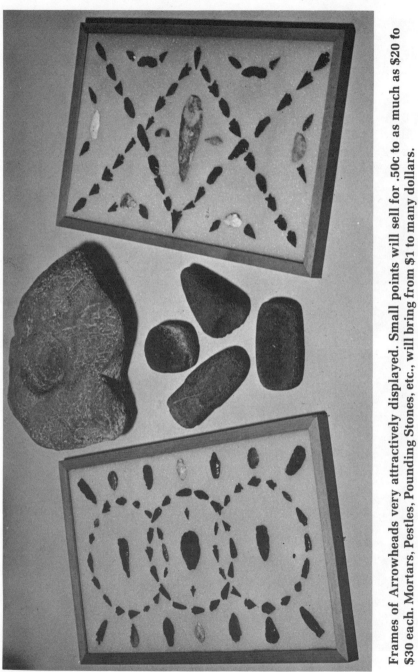

Frames of Arrowheads very attractively displayed. Small points will sell for .50c to as much as $20 to $30 each. Mortars, Pestles, Pounding Stones, etc., will bring from $1 to many dollars.

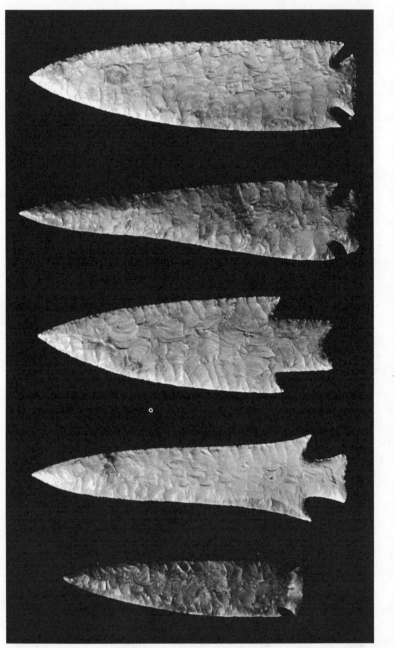

A nice group of Lance Heads. Good points bring a premium price. The group shown varies from eight inches to eleven and a half inches in length. The price range of this group is $65 for the smallest point to $150 for the largest one.

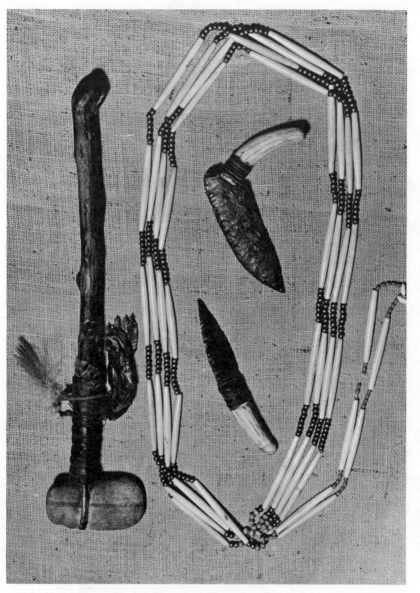

TOMAHAWK, BEADS and KNIVES—Fine Indian artifacts in this condition bring a very good price and are an asset to any collection.

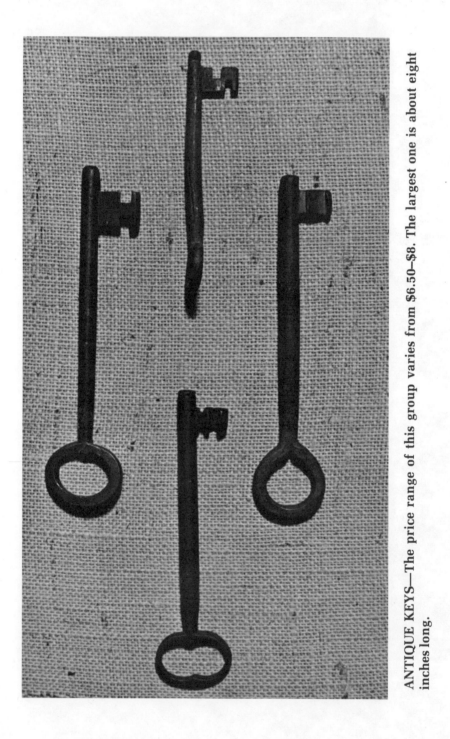

ANTIQUE KEYS—The price range of this group varies from $6.50–$8. The largest one is about eight inches long.

COW BELLS—Price range of this group is $1.50–$7.50.

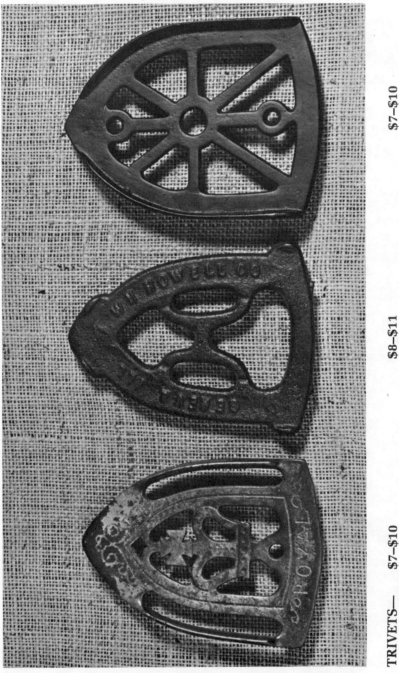

$7-$10

$8-$11

TRIVETS— $7-$10

FLAT IRONS AND SAD IRONS—Price range from $5–$25.

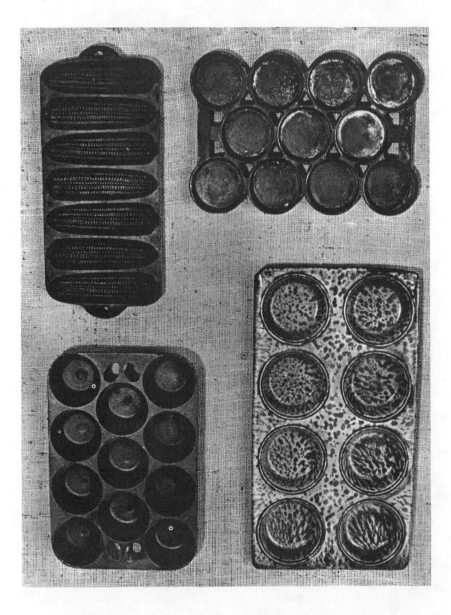

MUFFIN PANS—Price range of this group is $3.50–$10.

COOKING POTS AND UTENSILS

The price of the pots are: $12–$15 for the large one, $30–$40 for the small one, which is copper. The Utensils are priced from $2–$3.

OLD COFFEE POTS AND TEA KETTLE

The prices on Coffee Pots and Tea Kettles should range from $3–$15. Rare ones will bring more.

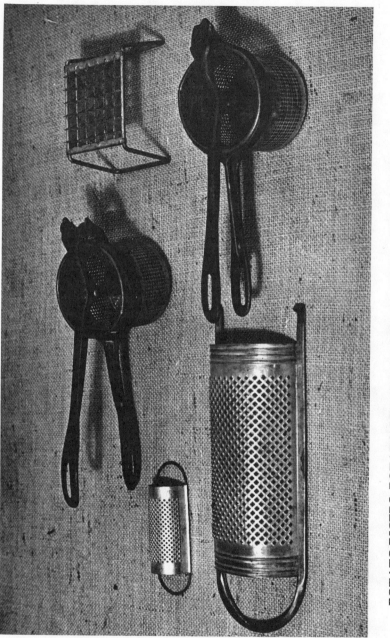

POTATO RICERS, POTATO GRATER, NUTMEG GRATER and POTATO CUTTER
Prices range from $3–$5 for the ricers and $1–$2 for the graters and cutter.

APPLE PEELER—$7.50–$15

COFFEE GRINDER—$7.50–$12.50

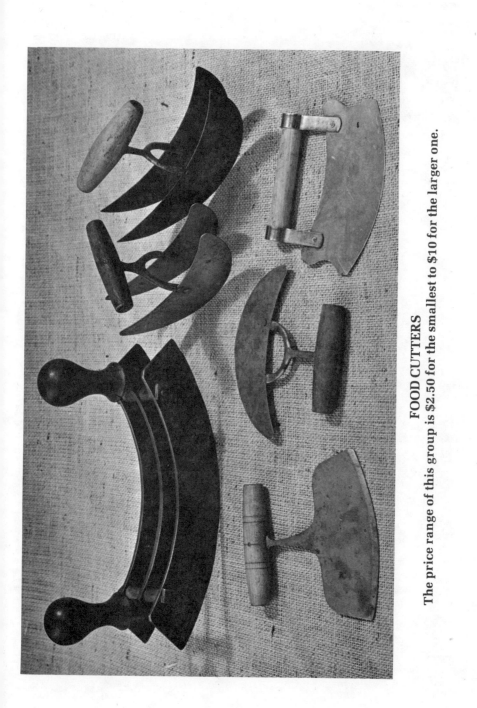

FOOD CUTTERS

The price range of this group is $2.50 for the smallest to $10 for the larger one.

A NICE GROUP OF KEROSENE LAMPS. The lamp at far right is a reconditioned Student Lamp—Patent 1871. The price of the Student Lamp should be $100–$125. The Curling Iron in the first lamp should bring $1–$3. The Kerosene Lamps should bring $20–$30 each.

LANTERNS—$15–$20 $4–$6 $8–$10

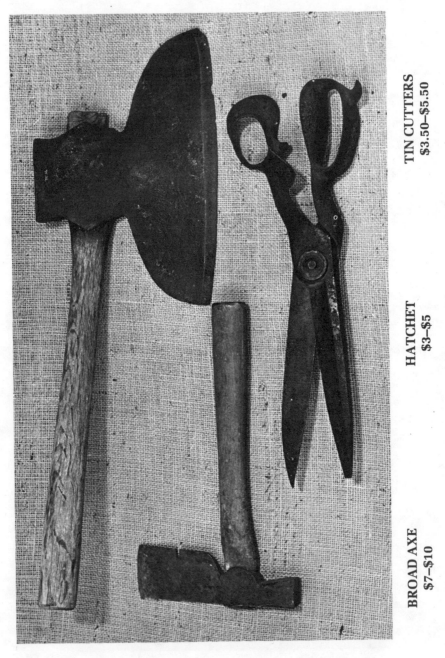

TIN CUTTERS
$3.50–$5.50

HATCHET
$3–$5

BROAD AXE
$7–$10

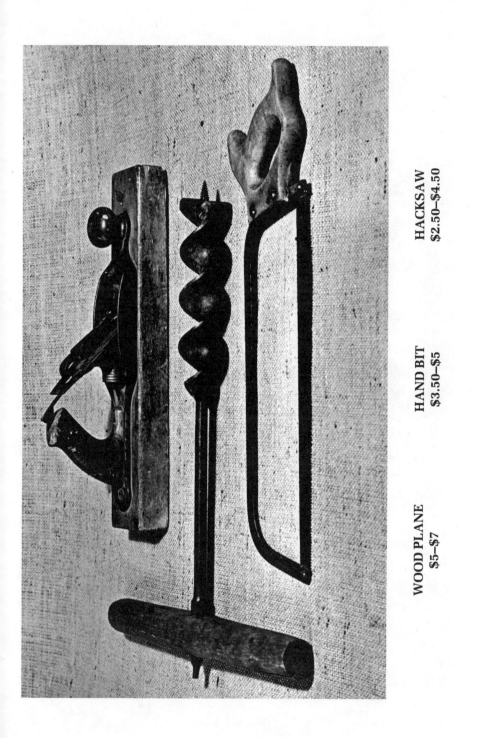

WOOD PLANE
$5—$7

HAND BIT
$3.50—$5

HACKSAW
$2.50—$4.50

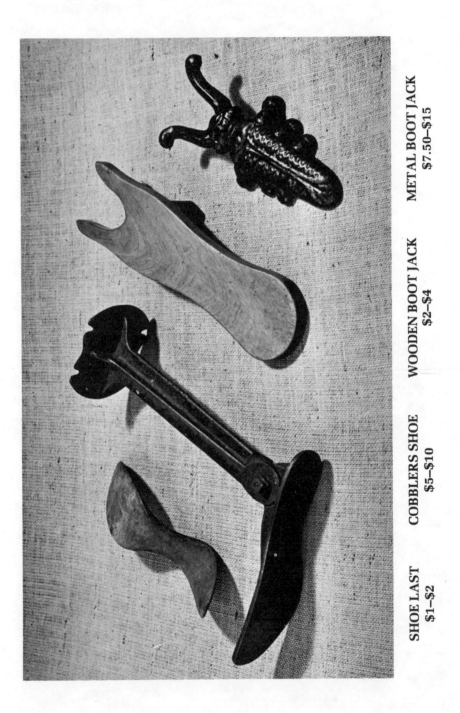

SHOE LAST $1-$2   COBBLERS SHOE $5-$10   WOODEN BOOT JACK $2-$4   METAL BOOT JACK $7.50-$15

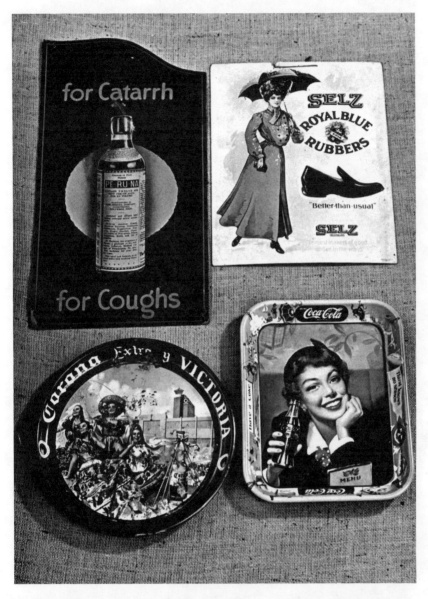

Display Signs, Posters and Beer and Soft Drink Trays are becoming very popular as collectors items. Signs and Trays will sell from $1–$50.

Antique Cans are very popular and bring anywhere from $2–$50 each.

Another nice group of cans. These cans are very colorful and can be arranged to form a very beautiful display in one's collection.

TOY SEWING MACHINES—$6.50–$15 each.

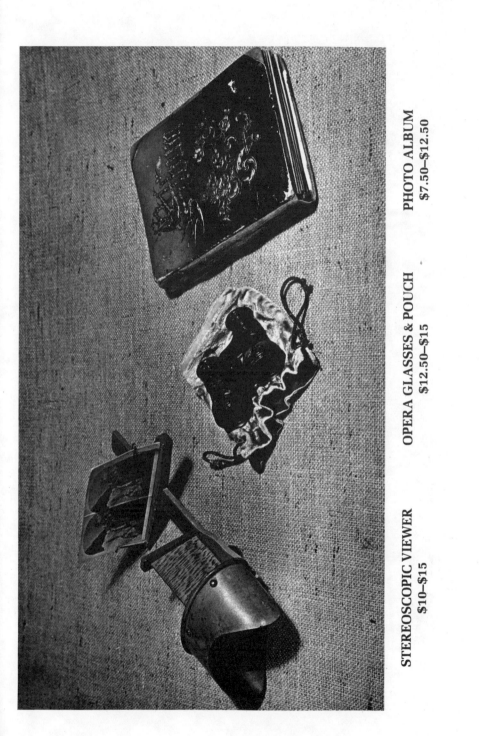

STEREOSCOPIC VIEWER
$10–$15

OPERA GLASSES & POUCH
$12.50–$15

PHOTO ALBUM
$7.50–$12.50

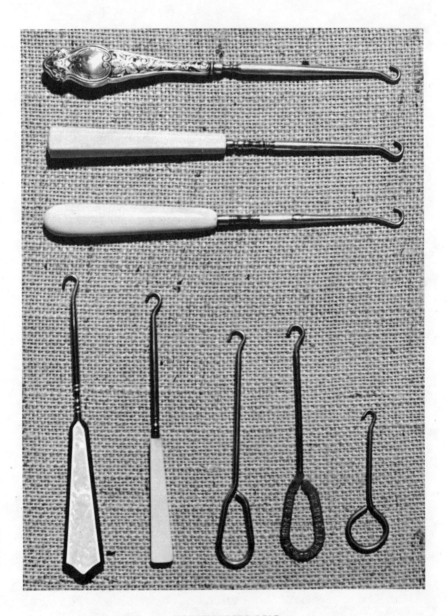

BUTTON HOOKS
The price of this group varies from .50c–$5 each.

FANS AND ORNAMENTAL COMBS
The Fans sell for $2–$15. The Combs sell for $10–$20.

[See page 149 for colorful illustration of Relics.]

INSULATORS

INSULATORS CAN BE FOUND in all shapes, sizes and colors and are giving Antique Bottles a run for their money in popularity. There are thousands of insulator collectors across the country and several good books have been written about them.

The prices on insulators have been making a steady climb over the last couple of years and I believe that they will go much higher. Prices on insulators will run anywhere from .50c to over $100.

I can't think of anything more beautiful than a well displayed collection of insulators. The color range is beyond description. Insulators have been around for a long time, well over a hundred years. Colors come in aqua, purple, green, yellow, amber, cobalt blue, milk glass, clear, carnival glass, brown, black, etc., and these colors run in all shades.

Some of the popular names to look for in insulators are Brookfield, Hemingray, Maydwell, Whitall Tatum, Cutter, Lowex, California, Gayner, Lynchburg, and Star, to name just a few.

Every once in a while you will read in the papers about bottle collectors being prosecuted for digging where they shouldn't, or undermining a road or building, or a treasure hunter being prosecuted for getting carried away and making like a Gopher in a city park. The insulator collector is certainly not to be left out. A few years ago we read an article in the paper about a couple of insulator collectors that were caught climbing telephone poles and exchanging new insulators for the old amethyst ones on the poles. A couple more collectors made the news by being caught cutting down saw-mill size Fir trees to get old insulators off of them. It's surprising to what lengths some collectors will go to add a piece to their collection.

On the following pages we have tried to cover a good variety of insulators and to photograph them in such a manner as to bring out their natural beauty. The prices quoted are in no way meant as the final word in pricing of these fine pieces, but represent what we consider to be a fair average being paid for these insulators. These prices will vary somewhat in different parts of the country.

[See pages 150-153 for additional illustrations of Insulators.]

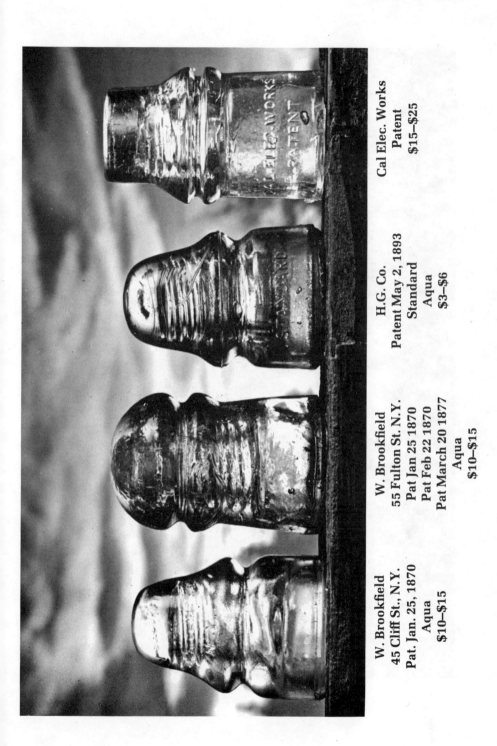

W. Brookfield
45 Cliff St., N.Y.
Pat. Jan. 25, 1870
Aqua
$10–$15

W. Brookfield
55 Fulton St. N.Y.
Pat Jan 25 1870
Pat Feb 22 1870
Pat March 20 1877
Aqua
$10–$15

H.G. Co.
Patent May 2, 1893
Standard
Aqua
$3–$6

Cal Elec. Works
Patent
$15–$25

Cutter
Pat Apr. 26 '04
Aqua
$25–$50

Pat'd
Nov 23'd 1886
Aqua
$5–$10

No Embossing
Lt. Green
$4–$6

No Embossing
Aqua
$5–$10

Postal
Dk. Yellow Green
$12–$15

Hemingray-43
Made in U.S.A.
Emerald Green
$5–$10

N.E.G.M. Co.
"Pat June 17 1890"
Green
$5–$10

Hemingray
No. 44
Aqua
$3–$8

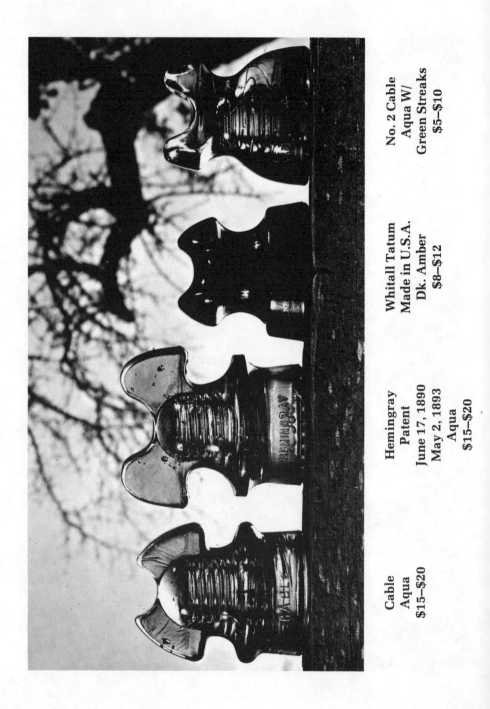

Cable
Aqua
$15–$20

Hemingray
Patent
June 17, 1890
May 2, 1893
Aqua
$15–$20

Whitall Tatum
Made in U.S.A.
Dk. Amber
$8–$12

No. 2 Cable
Aqua W/
Green Streaks
$5–$10

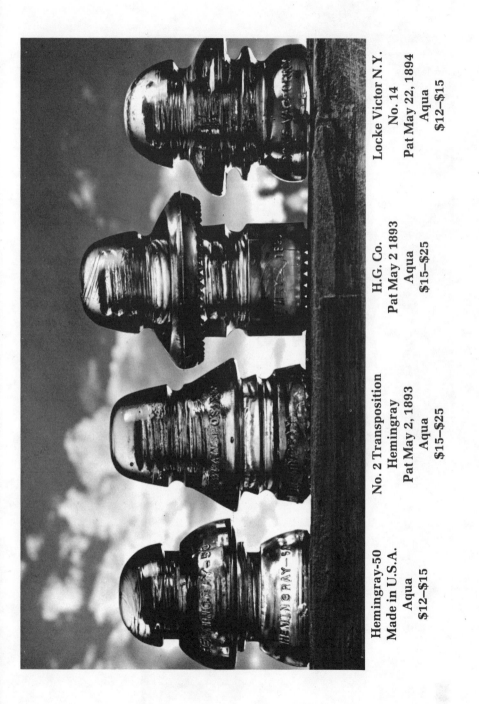

Hemingray-50
Made in U.S.A.
Aqua
$12–$15

No. 2 Transposition
Hemingray
Pat May 2, 1893
Aqua
$15–$25

H.G. Co.
Pat May 2 1893
Aqua
$15–$25

Locke Victor N.Y.
No. 14
Pat May 22, 1894
Aqua
$12–$15

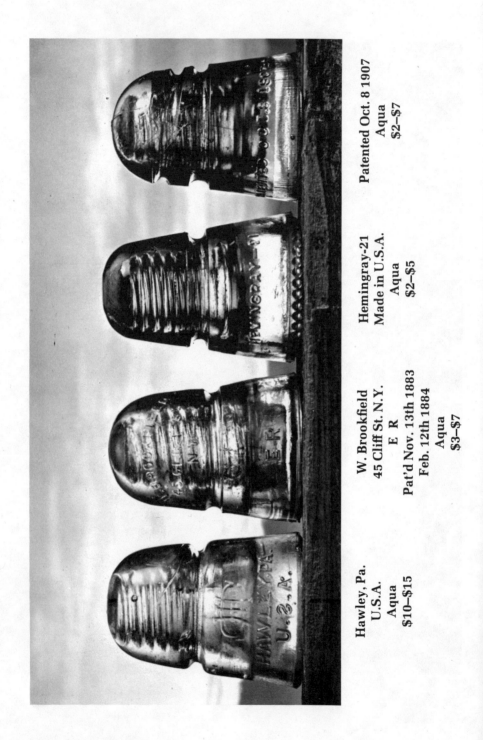

Hawley, Pa.
U.S.A.
Aqua
$10–$15

W. Brookfield
45 Cliff St. N.Y.
E R
Pat'd Nov. 13th 1883
Feb. 12th 1884
Aqua
$3–$7

Hemingray-21
Made in U.S.A.
Aqua
$2–$5

Patented Oct. 8 1907
Aqua
$2–$7

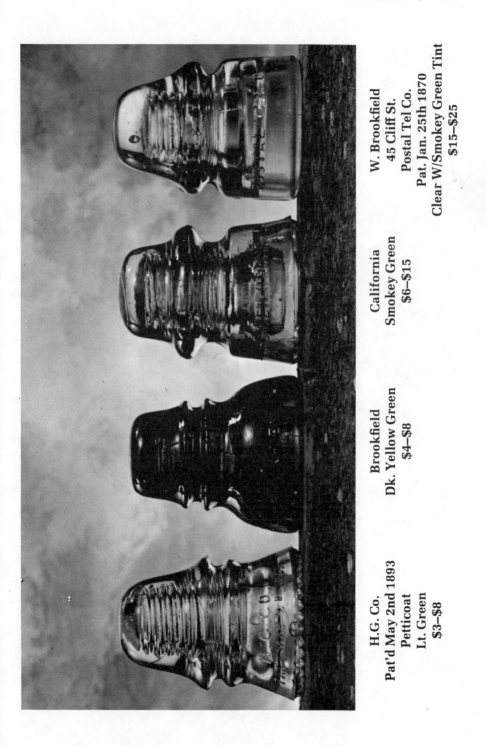

H.G. Co.
Pat'd May 2nd 1893
Petticoat
Lt. Green
$3–$8

Brookfield
Dk. Yellow Green
$4–$8

California
Smokey Green
$6–$15

W. Brookfield
45 Cliff St.
Postal Tel Co.
Pat. Jan. 25th 1870
Clear W/Smokey Green Tint
$15–$25

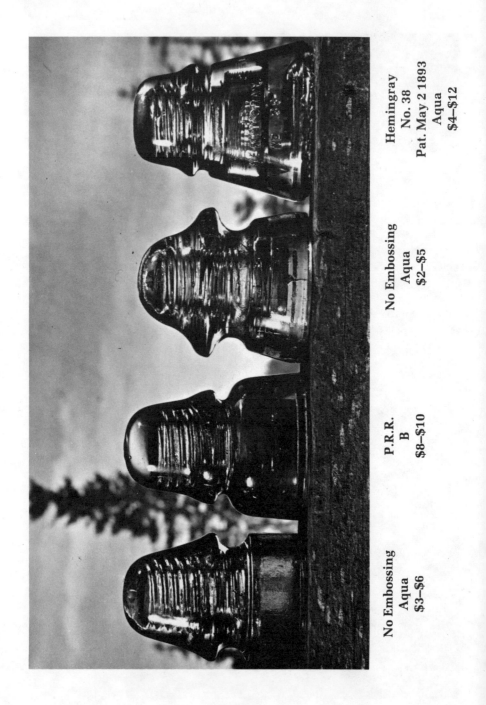

No Embossing
Aqua
$3–$6

P.R.R.
B
$8–$10

No Embossing
Aqua
$2–$5

Hemingray
No. 38
Pat. May 2 1893
Aqua
$4–$12

New Eng. Tel & Tel   Hemingray   Whitall Tatum Co. No. 1
       Aqua   Patent May 2nd 1893   Made in U.S.A.
      $3–$8   Muncie Type   Amethyst
                            Aqua $3–$8
                          $15–$35

California
Lt. Amethyst
$8–$10

Maydwell-14
U.S.A.
Lt. Amethyst
$2–$7

W. Brookfield
New York
Lt Green
$1–$3

W.G.M. Co.
Dark Amethyst
$12–$15

R. Good Jr.
Denver, Colo.
16
Aqua
$10–$15

B.T. Co.
Canada
Aqua
$7–$10

Gayner
No. 160
Aqua
$3–$7

Lynchburg
No. 30
Made in U.S.A.
Aqua
$3–$7

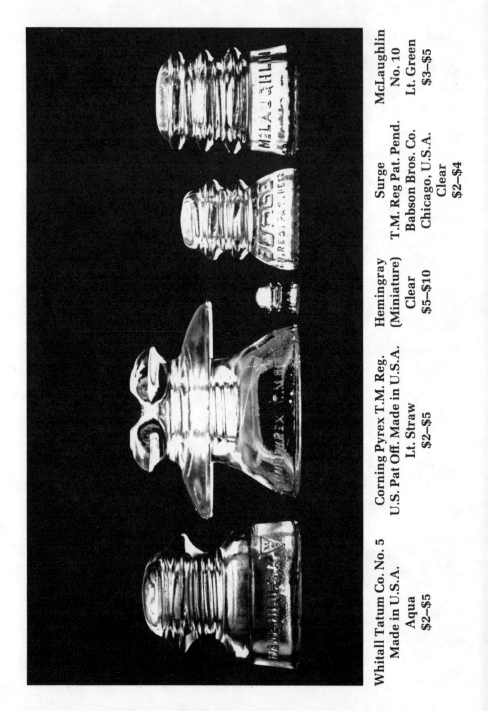

Whitall Tatum Co. No. 5
Made in U.S.A.
Aqua
$2–$5

Corning Pyrex T.M. Reg.
U.S. Pat Off. Made in U.S.A.
Lt. Straw
$2–$5

Hemingray
(Miniature)
Clear
$5–$10

Surge
T.M. Reg Pat. Pend.
Babson Bros. Co.
Chicago, U.S.A.
Clear
$2–$4

McLaughlin
No. 10
Lt. Green
$3–$5

[See pages 150-153 for additional illustrations of Insulators.]

TREASURE HUNTING

DID YOU KNOW THAT there's a modern day gold rush going on? Well there is, and you can get in on it. With the use of a metal detector anyone can find the countless small treasures that litter the land. Some of the luckier treasure hunters are actually finding buried treasure. A good metal detector, a little luck and perseverance can pay off.

The metal detector has been around for quite a few years but has really become popular within the last decade. This is becoming one of the most popular hobbies in the country and is certainly a hobby that usually more than pays for itself. Today there are quite a number of treasure hunting clubs across the country and new ones being formed every day.

There are dozens of good metal detectors on the market, with prices starting at less than twenty dollars and running to as high as several hundred dollars.

Most people ask the question, where can I use a detector? My answer is any place where there has been large gatherings of people for many years: Parks, carnival grounds, circus grounds, beaches, ball parks, forts, ghost towns, old homesteads, mines, etc. There is no limit. Its always a good idea to get permission before using one on private land, as well as parks, etc. You should also use care when digging. There is no need to deface property. You should leave the area in the same condition you found it. A screw driver works very well for small items, such as coins, rings, jewelry etc.

I remember one of my most prized finds was an 1855-S quarter found at an old town site. I also found an 1850 dime and an 1839-O half dime, as well as several Chinese coins, an old Spanish coin, jewelry and relics. That was quite a day. Last summer we found several hundred dollars worth of old coins and jewelry in our local park, which is around 100 years old. There have been several gold coins found in this park also.

If you're a shy type of person you may as well get over it because when using a detector in a park or anywhere there are people, you will have a curious crowd around you in a matter of minutes. It's a wonderful hobby the whole family can enjoy, and you'll love it.

No! the Goldmaster S-64 will not detect glass; however it will detect metals and minerals. Very few people in the old days bothered to separate cans, lids and glass, so they are usually found altogether. The metal detector is able to react to jar lids, barbed wire, spent shells, etc. Often a spent shell on a battle field will lead the collector to arrowheads as well, because where one rests, so does the other.

The young lady uses a COINMASTER IV around an old cabin, looking for coins. This lightweight sensitive instrument was especially designed for ladies because they don't get so tired after a little TH'ing. She didn't find anything of value that day, but there is always the next weekend!

The author and his wife are avid Treasure Hunters, as well as bottle collectors. Here the author uses a metal detector on a river beach in Southern Oregon.

Joe Martin, avid treasure hunter of Salem, Oregon, shows a weekend's take. Joe spends just about every weekend at old parks and school grounds coin shooting. He has one room full of relics, coins, bottles and artifacts.

Pictured here are some of the coins, jewelry, etc., found by the author and his wife during a recent summer. This was accumulated in just a few weekends. Many of the coins are quite rare. These small treasures were found with the two detectors pictured here. Treasure Hunting is one of the most relaxing and rewarding hobbies there is.

This set of silver and gold medals are part of the old Spanish treasure which was mined in Arizona by the Conquistadors and shipped home to Spain; however, much of it never reached the ships. The Yaqui Indians were the slave labor which labored in the hot mines and their heirs know where most of the remaining treasures lie. This is one TH'ing venture which no one should undertake without their help.

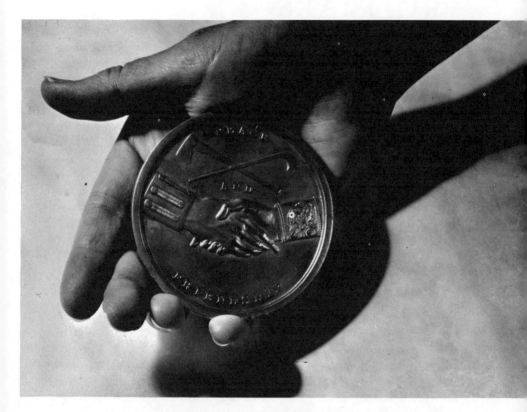

This "Peace and Friendship" medal was located in Montana with one of White's metal detectors. It is one of 12 which President Thomas Jefferson gave to Lewis and Clark when they made their famous trip to explore the Louisiana Purchase Territory. Eight of these medals have been located, usually in Indian Burial grounds when they were moved. The major Chiefs were given these lovely medallions.

FRUIT JARS

ONE OF THE MOST POPULAR phases of bottle collecting is Fruit Jars. This hobby got its start just a few years ago and is building up steam fast. Fruit Jars have been found in many different colors, ranging from aqua, green, amethyst, amber, etc. I have heard of some rare finds being made in cobalt blue and black glass but have yet to see one of these. There is a Kerr Fruit Jar commemorating the 65th anniversary, that is done with a gold finish.

Many people are under the impression that there were not very many variations of fruit jars manufactured, but there were over 400 different variations. Many different seals were used on fruit jars. Wax, glass, zinc, and tin were some of the most common.

The price of fruit jars will cost the collector anywhere from .50c to over $100 today. The price of a fruit jar, like bottles, may vary quite a bit depending on what part of the country you live in.

The fruit jar came into the picture in 1858 and was patented by John L. Mason, a young man 26 years of age. He was born in New Jersey and was living in New York at the time. John Mason's contribution to the food packing industry has to be rated as one of the greatest inventions of all time.

About five years ago my wife and I were excavating an old cabin that we had discovered in the woods east of Ashland. We were digging through the dried evergreen needles and rotting planks that used to be the floor. We were finding old flat irons, tools, bottles, etc. All of a sudden the shovel clinked against glass, so I reached down and raked the needles aside, which exposed an old aqua colored fruit jar. The zinc lid was still sealed and the jar contained Cherries, remarkably preserved. I would estimate that it had been at least 75 years since they had been canned. We couldn't help but wonder, who was the person that had canned this fruit so many years ago?

The Popularity of Fruit Jars has sky rocketed in the last couple of years. The Jars in this photo are all premium specimens.

Grandmother didn't know that those jars she was canning in would be so valuable some day. The starting price on any one of the jars in this group should be at least $15.

Another fine group of Fruit Jars. Note the one at the extreme right with Oriental Embossing.

A beautiful group of Amber colored Fruit Jars. The price range on these Fruit Jars can run anywhere from $25–$50 or possibly even higher.

Relics, relics, and relics! Pictured here are just a few, indicating the range of different relics that can be found—for those willing to really search them out.

[See pages 90–121 for additional illustrations and introduction to Relics.]

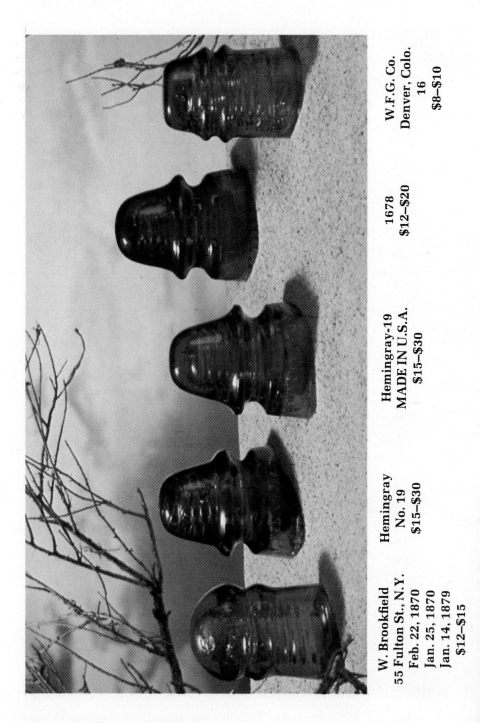

W. Brookfield
55 Fulton St., N.Y.
Feb. 22, 1870
Jan. 25, 1870
Jan. 14, 1879
$12–$15

Hemingray
No. 19
$15–$30

Hemingray-19
MADE IN U.S.A.
$15–$30

1678
$12–$20

W.F.G. Co.
Denver, Colo.
16
$8–$10

[See pages 122-134 for additional illustrations
and introduction to Insulators.]

No. 48
$3–$5

Corning Pyrex T.M. Reg. U.S.
Pat. Off. Made in U.S.A. 662
$20–$35

Maydwell-20
U.S.A.
$15–$30

No Embossing
$2–$5

Brooks Patent C.P.R.R.
Aug. 6, 1867
$35–$50

W.G.M. Co.
$12–$20

Lowex
Reg. U.S. Pat. Off.
512
11-Made in U.S.A.-0
$5–$15

E.C.&M. Co.
S.F.
$20–$30

(1 Star)
$3–$5

AM Tel & Tel Co.
$5–$12

(1-Star)
$3–$6

Duquesne. Glass Co.
Duquesne. G. Co.
$15–$20

Mulford & Biddle
$25–$50

W.U.T. Co.
Cauvets Pat
W Brookfield
Feb. 22-70
No. 55 Fulton St. N.Y.
$12–$18

C.G.I. Co.
$3–$8

[See pages 122-134 for additional illustrations
and introduction to Insulators.]

TOBACCO TINS

ONE OF THE FASTER GROWING hobbies in the country is tin container collecting. These beautiful collector's items played just as important a part in our colorful history as the glass containers, and therefore should be every bit as highly regarded by the collector. They should be preserved for our future generations to enjoy.

The variety one finds in these old tins is almost as great as found in the glass containers. One of the most popular types of tin containers is the tobacco tins, which come in all shapes, sizes and colors. The large store tins are probably the most impressive. These usually held about 48 cakes, or plugs, of tobacco and were quite colorful and lavishly decorated. Some of the brands that were packed into these large containers were Sure Shot, Game, Tiger, Sweet Mist, Sweet Cuba, and Beachnut, to name just a few.

The lunch box type tobacco tins are one of the most popular types of the tobacco tins. These came compete with wire handle for carrying, and were used by many children from the late 1800's to the 1940's, for packing their lunches to school. Dozens of different brands of tobacco were packed in these lunch box type tins, giving the collector plenty of variety in this type of container. Some of the other types of tobacco tins to watch for are the round canister type, the round pail type, with wire handle, and the assorted smaller sizes. The round pail type was also used for lunch buckets.

These tins were used for many things, as well as lunch boxes. They were handy for storing nuts and bolts, needles and thread, buttons, money, matches, marbles, jewelry, photos, etc. Many of these old tins can still be found in the old barns and buildings across the country, covered with dust and still holding nails or nuts and bolts, or maybe in the attic still holding some old treasures of long ago. As this hobby becomes more popular there are many of these beautiful old containers showing up in our antique and relic shops across the country.

The prices on tins, like bottles or any other collectible will vary somewhat in different parts of the country. We have written hundreds of letters and purchased many tins from all over the country, and feel that the prices quoted in this book are a fairly accurate average of what these tins are selling for across the country.

Many of the tins that you find will be bent and rusty but a little pressure applied carefully in the right spots will remove a lot of the dents, and a little mild soap applied with a damp cloth and then some spray wax, or in some cases, spray lacquer, will restore them quite nicely.

Some rust and small dents are acceptable as it is hard to find tins in like new condition. Tobacco tins in like new condition, like coins in mint condition, will bring a slightly higher price than tins just in good to very good condition. The prices quoted in this book are for tins in good to very good condition, for instance a Union Leader lunch box type tin would be priced at $8-$12. This means you would pay around $8 for this tin in good condition, or $12 for the same tin in very good condition. The price would be lower than $8 if the tin were in poor to fair condition, or might be a little higher than $12 if the tin was in like new appearance.

Some tins are quite rare and hard to find, while others are quite common and easy to locate. After you collect tobacco tins for awhile you will become aware of which ones are common and which ones are rare. This is when the hobby really becomes interesting, because at this point you really start to search in earnest for those rare tins that really appeal to you. There are still thousands of rare tins to be purchased across the country, and many more to be found under the old buildings, in the attics, barns and many other places where they have been thrown or stored.

We hope with this book that we have been able, in some small way, to help kindle more interest in these beautiful pieces of our historically wonderful past.

$25–$50 $35–$60

$75–$100

$25–$50 $20–$35

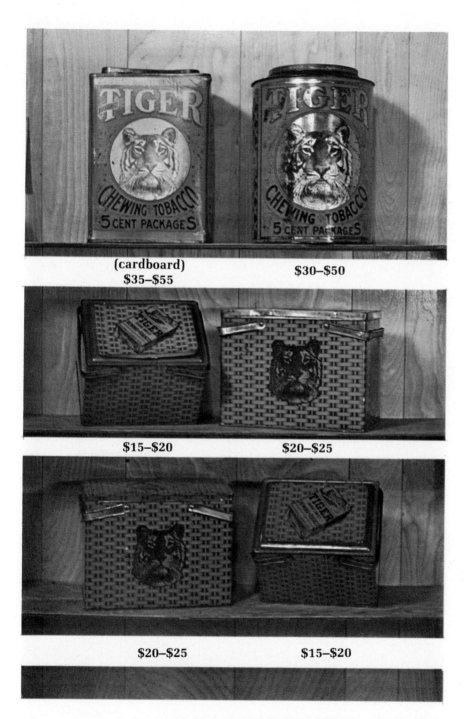

(cardboard)
$35–$55

$30–$50

$15–$20

$20–$25

$20–$25

$15–$20

[See page 177 for introduction to Store Tins.]

$30–$40 $15–$25 $10–$15

$35–$60 $10–$15 $35–$60

$15–$25 $35–$65 $15–$25

[See page 178 for introduction to Lunch Box Tins.]

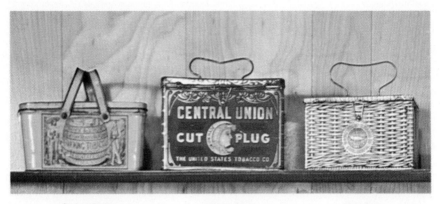

$10–$15 $25–$35 $7–$12

$15–$20 $7–$12 $10–$20

$25–$40 $10–$15 $10–$25

$25–$45 $50–$100 $35–$45

(telescoping) $7–$12 $8–$12
$35–$50

$20–$35 $10–$15 $20–$35

[See page 178 for introduction to Lunch Box Tins.]

$15–$25 $15–$30   (paper label)
                                  $15–$25

$25–$50 $75–$100 $20–$35

$15–$30 $35–$55 $5–$10

[See page 179 for introduction to Round Pail and Canister Tins.]

$10–$20 $25–$40 $5–$10

(cigars)   (cigars) $10–$20
$15–$30 $10–$20

$5–$10 $5–$10 $7–$12 $20–$35

[See page 179 for introduction to Round Pail and Canister Tins.]

$3–$5 $3–$5 $4–$6

$3–$5 $8–$10 $2–$4

$2–$4 $5–$7 $6–$8

[See page 180 for introduction to Pocket and Sample Tins.]

$1–$2 $1–$2 $3–$5

$3–$5 $2–$3 $3–$5

(cardboard) $2–$3 $5–$7
$6–$10

50c–$1   50c–$1   50c–$1

50c–$1   50c–$1   50c–$1

50c–$1   50c–$1   50c–$1

[See page 180 for introduction to Pocket and Sample Tins.]

$5–$10 $2–$4 $5–$7

$4–$6 $4–$6 $4–$6

$3–$5 $6–$8 $5–$7

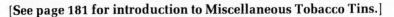

[See page 181 for introduction to Miscellaneous Tobacco Tins.]

$5–$7 $4–$6 $5–$7

$6–$8 $4–$6 $4–$6

$5–$7 $1–$3 $3–$5

$2–$4 $4–$6 $3–$5

(metal sign) $2–$4
$5–$10

$2–$3 $6–$10 $3–$4 $2–$3

$10–$12 $6–$8

$4–$6 $5–$7 $2–$3

$3–$5 $6–$10

$4–$7 $5–$10 $15–$25

$20–$35 $15–$20   (paper label)
                                            $8–$12

$10–$15 $15–$20 $75–$125

$20–$30 $6–$10 $10–$15

$15–$30   (cigars) $20–$35
                  $25–$40

$6–$10 $10–$15 $8–$15

$5–$10 $5–$10 $5–$8

$5–$8 $5–$8 $6–$10

$6–$10 $3–$6 $6–$10

$12–$15 $3–$5 $15–$20

$3–$5 $6–$10 $3–$5

$4–$6 $8–$10

$3–$5 $8–$10

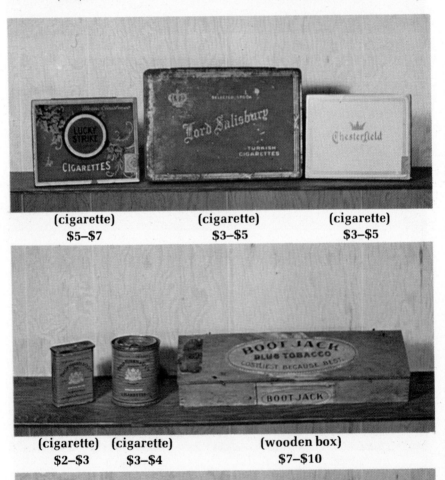

(cigarette)   (cigarette)   (cigarette)
$5–$7 $3–$5 $3–$5

(cigarette)   (cigarette)   (wooden box)
$2–$3 $3–$4 $7–$10

Cloth and paper pouches. Prices on these will be anywhere from 50c–$1 for the common ones, to $3–$6 for the less common ones.

[See page 181 for introduction to Miscellaneous Tobacco Tins.]

STORE TINS

THE LARGE STORE TINS are the hardest to find because there were not as many of these manufactured. These tins usually held 48 cakes, or plugs of tobacco and were usually displayed on the counter of the old tobacco store or anywhere they sold tobacco. Many of these store tins will have colorful pictures or designs on the inside of the lid. This made an attractive display when the lid was open. The store tins come in many shapes and sizes. Some of these store containers were made of cardboard with a tin top and bottom, but most of them were completely made of tin.

Prices on the large tins will vary anywhere from $10 to as much as $60, depending on condition, rarity and location where purchased. One of the most common of the store tins is the Tiger Tin, which can be found in round and rectangular shapes. These are a beautiful tin picturing a Tiger's head on the sides. The Tiger tins can be found in red or blue. Probably the most attractive of these are the large round ones which come in red with gold and black lettering and pictures a large Tiger's head in a circle on the side.

One of the harder ones to obtain is Sure Shot, which is rectangular, and pictures an Indian drawing a bow. Sweet Mist and Game are also quite hard to find. I am sure that there are many brands that we have not yet seen or heard of, that will show up in the future. One thing is for sure, these large tins are worth investing in when you find them.

[See pages 156-157 for illustrations of Store Tins.]

LUNCH BOX TINS

ONE OF THE MOST POPULAR of the tobacco tins is the lunch box type. I don't know how many different brands of tobacco were packed in these, but there seems to be much variety in this type of container. The lunch box tins came with a wire handle and latch on the side or end. The size will vary considerably. As recently as the 1940's many lunches were packed to school in these colorful containers. No doubt many of you can remember carrying your lunch in one.

Some of the more common names were George Washington, Union Leader, Pedro and Dixie Queen. Some of the harder ones to find are Winner, Fashion, Dixie Kid and Brotherhood.

Winner was manufactured by the American Tobacco Co. as recently as 1949. Fashion was manufactured by a predecessor of the American Tobacco Co. in 1855 and was manufactured by the American Tobacco Co. until 1952. They discontinued the Fashion lunch box pail in 1943.

Prices on the lunch box tins will vary from $5 to as much as $35 for the rare ones. Age does not play as important a part in determining the price of a tin as availability. Many tins that were manufactured as recently as the 1940's will bring much more than some tins manufactured 50 years earlier. As with coins, the value is determined by the number that was minted, more than it is by the age. This holds true for Tobacco Tins as well as any other collectible, rarity is the first thing to consider. Some tins that were manufactured as recently as the early 1950's are very desirable.

I believe that we are going to see a lot more of the tin containers at the antique and bottle shows and on the shelves in the shops, as this type of collecting comes into its own. I have heard that there are already some clubs being formed by tin container collectors, and by the letters that we have received it would appear that this hobby is really starting to build up steam. When you start your collection remember that these lunch box tins offer lots of variety and represent a good investment.

[See pages 158-160 for illustrations of Lunch Box Tins.]

ROUND PAIL AND CANISTER TINS

THE ROUND PAIL TYPE tobacco tins also had a wire handle and were used as lunch boxes. These tins also come in many varieties, including many with paper labels. Many of these tins resemble a lard bucket in appearance.

Most of the tobacco companies packed their products in several different sizes and types of tins. For example you can find Dixie Queen, Union Leader, Pedro, Sweet Cuba and George Washington to name just a few, in the lunch box, canister and several smaller sizes. It really enhances one's collection if he can obtain the different sizes of each tin.

The canister or humidor tins are very interesting, as many of these were designed to be sold as gifts and were usually lavishly decorated and quite colorful. Humidor tins can be found in square and rectangular shapes, as well as round. Some of these have fancy little handles or knobs on the lid, which tends to enhance their appearance. The pail and canister tins are very popular and no collection should be without them.

[See pages 161-162 for illustrations of Round Pail and Canister Tins.]

POCKET AND SAMPLE TINS

IF VARIETY IS YOUR CUP OF TEA then these small tins are for you, because they seem to come in endless shapes, sizes and colors. The pocket tins were designed to fit into your shirt pocket for handy carrying. These little tins, like the larger ones, are very colorful and attractive.

Many of the brands have long been discontinued, while many are still being packed and sold in tins almost identical to the ones from fifty or sixty years ago. The sample tins were usually designed very similar to the larger tins, and were given away, or sold, by the tobacco companies to advertise their tobaccos. The tobacco salesman usually always had a plentiful supply of these small tins to use in promoting his company's product.

These small tins are very attractive and require little room to display. If you would like to start collecting tobacco tins, but have little space for showing, you might consider these small sample tins.

Many bottle collectors collect only miniatures due to lack of space, so this should work just as well with sample tins, so why not start your collection now? It's a great hobby!, and you'll love it.

[See pages 163-165 for illustrations of Pocket and Sample Tins.]

MISCELLANEOUS TOBACCO TINS

MISCELLANEOUS TOBACCO TINS are illustrated on pages 166 to 175. These come in many different sizes, shapes and colors. The variety is almost endless. Some of the harder ones to find are the Fast Mail, Green Seal, Canuck, North Star, Madeira and Arcadia.

Many brands of tobacco were packed in several different sizes and shapes of tins, for instance you may find the George Washington brand in the lunch box, the round canister, the small lunch box type, with and without the wire handle, and in the small pocket tin. The canister type also came in a large and a small size. To acquire the different sizes of each brand makes an interesting collection.

With tin collecting you may find that you will be able to upgrade your collection considerably as you go along. You may find an interesting tin, but it will only be in fair condition, and at a later date find another like it in very good condition, with which you will want to replace the first one. The duplicates that you acquire from upgrading can be used for trading stock, or you can sell them.

There are many different ways in which one can build a beautiful collection and we hope we have been able to help with this book. The rest is up to you.

[See pages 166-175 for illustrations of Miscellaneous Tobacco Tins.]

TOBACCO
ADVERTISING

ON THE FOLLOWING PAGES are photos of tobacco advertisements, trade cards, signs & posters, all very collectable pieces of early day America. These colorful old signs and posters tend to enhance one's collection when displayed with it, especially when you are fortunate enough to find signs advertising some of the same brands that you have in your collection.

Sometimes you will see a sign or poster advertising an interesting brand of tobacco, and this will start you on a search to try to locate a tin that held that particular brand of tobacco. This is just another one of the many enjoyments derived from tobacco tin collecting.

The price range on these old signs and posters will range from a few dollars to as high as fifty dollars, if you are lucky enough to find them, and then even luckier in persuading the party to sell them to you.

The old signs were usually printed on a heavy cardboard, but can also be found on tin and even wood. Next time you are making the rounds in search of new tins for your collection, see if you can find any of these old signs or posters. They are not easy to find, but if you do, they are definitely worthy of adding to your collection.

Old building with tobacco advertisement still visible.

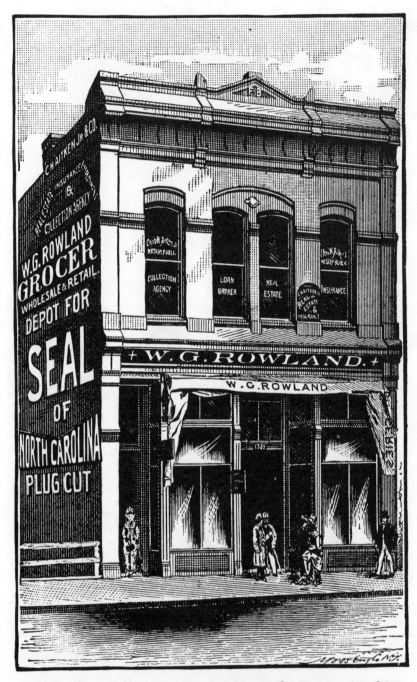

Sketch from 1888 newspaper. Caption reads, Tacoma Washington Territory, 1888. Note the tobacco sign on the side of the building.

Old Tobacco sign. These signs are usually very colorful, and are highly collectable.

Nice heavy cardboard sign.

Tin Sign (very colorful).

Many of the tobacco companies put out colorful little trade cards which had cartoons or pictures on one side and advertised their product on the other side. These little cards are highly collectible and go very well with a collection of tins and posters. Pictured is a set of these cards. A good way to display these is to put them in long narrow frames and place them around your tin collection. Trade cards, signs, flags, advertisements, etc., tend to add to one's tin collection.

1895 Tobacco Ad

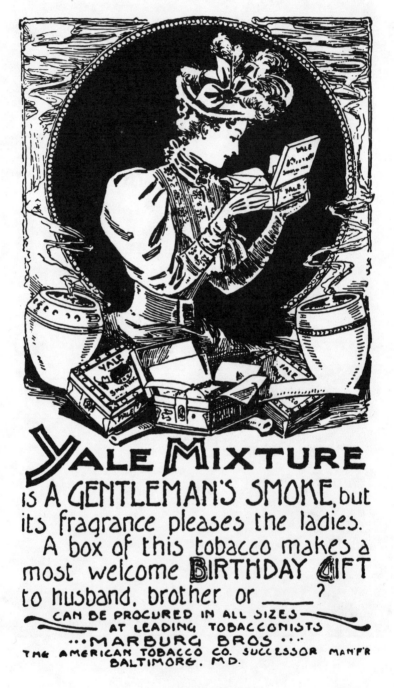

1895 Tobacco Ad

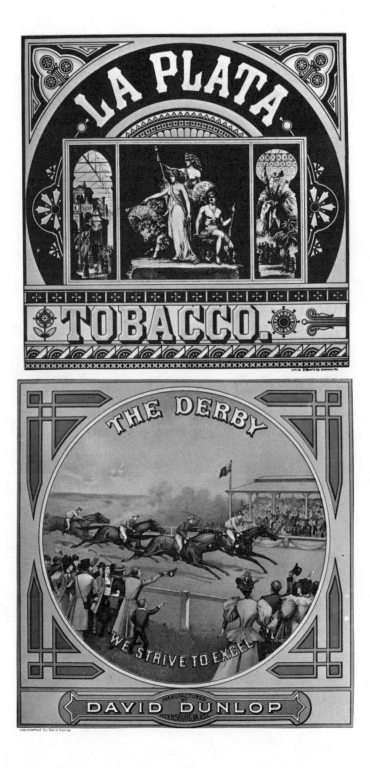

Tobacco Cutters and Thermometer tobacco sign. Tobacco Cutters usually sell for $10–$35, signs will sell for $5–$100.

A nice display with sign, tins and cutter.

INDEX

BOTTLES

BEERS, WINES AND ALES
California Bottling Co.   /   52, 53
Cambrinus Bottling Co.   /   53
Claus Wreden Brewing Co.   /   53
El Dorado Brewing Co.   /   52
Etna Brewery   /   40
Gde Chartreuse   /   42
John Rapp & Son   /   53
Lion Brewery Ltd.   /   53
Montebello Wine   /   56
Palmtag, A. & Co.   /   52
Pottery Ale   /   35, 88
St. Helena Bottling Co.   /   52
Stroh Brewing Co.   /   52
Wine (unembossed)   /   82

BITTERS
Abbott & Co., C.W.   /   71
Atwood's   /   32
Baxter's Dr.   /   32
Caroni   /   32
Cassin's   /   33
Clark's   /   34
Crown   /   71
Damiana   /   34
Doyles   /   71
Electric   /   41, 71, 74
Ernst L. Arp & Kiel   /   32
Excelsior   /   33, 73
Harters, Dr.   /   72
Henley's, Dr.   /   33
Hostetter's, Dr. J.   /   36, 73
Ladies Leg   /   72
Langley's, Dr.   /   34
Lash's   /   32, 33, 36, 41, 73, 74
Peruvian   /   72
Prickly Ash   /   33, 41, 73
Siegert & Hijos   /   32
St. Drakes   /   71

JIM BEAMS
Alaska Purchase   /   27
Antioch   /   28
Antique Trader, The   /   26
Black Katz   /   30
Blue Cherub (1960)   /   31
Blue Daisy   /   65
Broadmoor   /   27

Cable Car   /   66
Cameo Blue   /   66
Cats   /   64
Cheyenne Cent.   /   27
Cleopatra—Yellow   /   66
Delft Blue   /   66
Donkeys   /   63, 64
Eagle   /   30
Elephants   /   63, 64
Fox   /   30
Green China Jug   /   65
Harold's Club Blue Slot   /   29
Harold's Club Pin Wheel   /   29
Hawaii   /   25
Hemisphere   /   29
Idaho   /   23
Illinois   /   24
Kentucky   /   24, 25
Kentucky Cardinal   /   29
Laramie, Wyo.   /   28
Majestic (1966)   /   31
Marbled Fantasy (1965)   /   31
Marina City   /   26
Nebraska   /   25
New Hampshire   /   25
New Jersey   /   23
New Mexico   /   26
New York Worlds Fair   /   65
Ohio   /   24
Oregon   /   23
Pennsylvania   /   24
Pony Express   /   28
Prestige (1967)   /   31
Price Listings:
    Centennial Series   /   67
    Customer Specialties   /   68
    Executive Series   /   67
    Glass Specialties   /   69
    Political Series   /   67
    Regal China Specialties   /   69
    State Series   /   67
    Trophy Series   /   68
Redwood   /   28
Royal Rose (1963)   /   31
Ruby Crystal   /   65
San Diego   /   27
Seattle Worlds Fair   /   29
Smoked Crystal   /   66
Turquoise Jug   /   65
West Virginia   /   23

Yellow Katz / 30
Yosemite / 26
Zimmerman (1968) / 30

**MEDICINE AND
CONDIMENT BOTTLES**
Acid Bottle / 76
Ayer's Hair Vigor / 79
Barrel Mustard / 40
Boericke & Schreck / 87
Boschee's, Dr. A., German
   Syrup / 80
Burnetts Cocoanine / 77
Chamberlains C.C. & D. Remedy / 86
Condiment Bottle / 42
Creomulsion / 81
Davis Vegetable Pain Killer / 86
Fellows & Co. Chemists / 80
Fitch, Drs. S.S. & Sons / 77
Hale, R.S. & Co. / 77
Hall's Catarrh Cure / 86
H.H.H. Horse Medicine / 41, 84
Hoff's German Liniment / 83
Holbrook & Co. / 22
Jane's, Dr. D., Tonic Vermifuge / 83
Katz & Besthoff Pharmacists / 77
Kennedy's, Dr., Medical
   Discovery / 80
Kilmer's, The Great Dr. Swamp
   Root / 81
Laxol / 79
Liquozone / 86
McLean, Dr., J. H. / 79
Medicines (unembossed) / 79, 87
Miles, Dr. / 80, 81
Morgan, E. & Sons / 42
Mothers Friend, The / 40, 84
Muegge The Druggist / 35
Pierce's, Dr., Golden Medical
   Discovery / 35, 81
Pinkham's, Lydia E. / 84
Potters, Mrs., Hygienic Supply / 87
Puritana / 42
Radway, R.R.R., & Co. / 77
Sanford's Radical Cure / 35, 76
Scott's Emulsion / 83
Sharp & Dohme / 87
Simmon's Liver Regulator / 45
Tonic Vermifuge / 84
Trask's, A., Magnetic Ointment / 79

Wakelee's Camelline / 79
Warner's Kidney & Liver Cure / 36, 42
Watkin's / 45
Waw Waw / 42
Wine of Cardui / 81
Wistars, Dr., Balsam / 35, 83
Wyeth & Bro. / 83

MISCELLANEOUS BOTTLES
Ayer's Sarsaparilla / 82
Bottles with Labels / 37
Carbona / 40, 76
Case Gin / 78
Chinese Jugs / 89
Damschinsky, C., Hair Dye / 87
Durkee's Challenge Sauce / 76
Extract Bottles / 40, 85
Gilka, J.A. / 72
Greers Washing Ammonia / 44
Hoboken, A van / 41
Ink Bottles / 76, 79
Johnston's Fluid Beef / 76
J. S. P. / 44
Lea & Perrins Worchestershire
   Sauce / 76
Olive Bottle / 76
Peppersauce Bottles / 35, 39, 82
Poison Bottles / 38, 87
Pottery Inks / 88
Roehling & Shultz / 72
Schiedam Voldner's Aromatic
   Schnapps / 78
Selick, C.H., Perfumer / 87
Shoe Polish / 40
Whittemore / 86

SODA AND MINERAL WATER
American Soda Works / 47
Ashland Lithia Springs / 40, 51
Bigham, P.C. / 82
Blob Top Soda / 40
C.O.D. Soda Works / 50
Crystal Carbonating Co. / 47
Eel River Valley Soda Works / 44, 46
Ebberwien, G., Ginger Ale / 44
Empire Soda Works / 48
Fargo Bottling Works Co. / 50
G.W. Angels / 47
Hippler & Bricksons / 49
Hot Springs Bottling Works / 47

Jackson's Napa Soda / 40, 45, 46, 51
John Ryan / 44, 46
John Ryan Excelsior / 44, 46
Johnson Liverpool / 78
Jurgens & Price Bottlers / 49
Merrill Soda Works / 40, 45, 51
M.F. & Co. / 44
Mineral Water / 47
North Western Bottling Co. / 49
Philipsburg Bottling Works / 48, 50
Pioneer Soda Works / 50
Pottery Mineral Water Bottles / 80
Samuel Soda Springs / 48
Santa Rosa Bottling Co. / 48
Saxlehner's Bitterquelle / 34
Siskiyou Natural Mineral Water / 51
Sodas (unembossed) / 35, 82
Tallman, G.W. / 49
Telluride Bottling Co. / 50
Upper Soda / 51
Waialua Soda Works Ltd. / 45
Whittakers Altham / 48
William's Bros. / 46
Witter Springs Water / 78

WHISKEY BOTTLES
Benz & Sons / 17
Blake's, G.O. / 55
Bonnie Bros. / 55
Brown Foreman Co. / 61
Chevalier Co. / 20
Ciacomini & Boyd / 56
Crown Dist. / 18
Cutter, J.F. / 17
Cutter, J.H. / 61
Cyrus Noble / 17, 59
Duffy / 21, 22, 74
Gordons Dry Gin / 58
Hall, Luhrs & Co. / 20, 22, 55, 60
Hannis Dist / 18
Hildebrandt Posner / 21
Homer's Calif. Ginger Brandy / 78
J. Rieger / 55
Jesse Moore / 20
L. T. & Co. / 54, 60
Levaggi Co. / 20, 22, 74
Lilienthal & Co. / 56
Louis Taussig & Co. / 55, 61
Moore, C.H. / 61

Neals Ambrosia / 18
Oregon Importing Co. / 56
Paul Jones / 18
Pepper Dist. / 58
Roth & Co. / 61
Siebe Bros & Plageman / 17
Van Schuyver, W.J. & Co. / 21, 60
Varwig, H. & Co. / 60
Wisseman, Geo. / 21, 74
Wright & Taylor / 54
Whiskies (no embossing) / 17, 19, 21, 22, 54, 56–58, 60

FRUIT JARS
Cohansey / 145
Gem / 147
Globe / 145, 146, 148
Lieng Hop & Co. / 147
Lighting / 148
Mason / 146, 147
Sun / 145–147
Woodbury / 145, 146

INSULATORS
Am. Tel. & Tel. Co. / 152
Brooks / 151
Brookfield / 123, 128, 129, 132, 15(
B. T. Co. / 133
Cable / 126
Cal. Elec. Works / 123
California / 129, 132
C.G.I. Co. / 153
Corning Pyrex / 134, 151
Cutter / 124
Duquesne Glass Co. / 153
E.C. & M. Co. / 152
Gayner / 133
Hawley, Pa. / 128
Hemingray / 125–128, 130, 131, 134, 150
H. G. Co. / 123, 127, 129
Locke Victor, N.Y. / 127
Lowex / 152
Lynchburg / 133
Maydwell / 132, 151
McLaughlin / 134
Mulford & Biddle / 153
N. E. G. M. Co. / 125
New England Tel. & Tel. / 131

Postal / 125
P. R. R. / 130
R. Good, Jr. / 133
Star / 152, 153
Surge / 134
Unembossed Insulators / 124, 128,
130, 150, 151
W. F. G. Co. / 150
W. G. M. Co. / 132, 152
Whitall Tatum / 126, 131, 134
W. U. T. Co. / 153

RELICS
Apple Peeler / 108
Boot Jacks, etc. / 114
Button Hooks / 120
Cans / 116, 117
Coffee Grinder / 108
Coffee Pots & Tea Kettle / 106
Cooking Pots & Utensils / 105
Cow Bells / 101
Fans / 121
Food Cutters / 109
Hand Guns / 92–96
Indian Relics / 97–99
Irons / 103
Keys / 100
Lamps / 110, 111
Muffin Pans / 104
Opera Glasses / 119
Ornamental Combs / 121
Photo Album / 119
Potato Ricers & Graters / 107
Powder Horns / 91
Stereoscopic Viewer / 119
Tools / 112, 113
Toy Sewing Machines / 118
Trays & Signs / 115, 149
Trivets / 102

TREASURE HUNTING / 135–143

TOBACCO

TOBACCO CUTTERS
Champion / 202
Climax / 202
Five Bro's. / 202
Penn / 203

TOBACCO SIGNS AND ADS
Black Swan / 195
Britannia / 196
Crusader / 197
Golden Sceptre / 191
Hot Ball / 187
Just The Thing / 194
Mail Pouch / 186
McRae / 193
Red Horse / 185
Sailor's Hope / 198
Welcome Nugget / 199
Yale Mixture / 192
Zadie / 200

TOBACCO TINS
Arcadia Mixture / 170
Babys Bottom / 166
Bagdad / 166
Beech Nut / 156
Belfast / 170, 172
Belwood / 167
Best / 171
Big Ben / 163
Bin 56 / 165
Boot Jack / 174
Brotherhood / 160
Brownie Tin-Mayo's / 170
Bull Dog / 163
Cake Box / 169
Canuck / 168
Central Union / 159
Chesterfield / 174
Cinco / 162
Climax / 168, 173, 174, 203
Climax Golden Twins / 173
Club Mixture / 165
Columbia / 161
Comet / 175
Cross Swords / 167
Crow-Mo-Smokers / 171
Dan Patch / 160, 172
Dial / 163
Dill's Best / 168, 170, 172
Dixie Kid / 160
Dixie Queen / 158, 160, 161
Don Porto / 162
Durham / 175
Edgeworth / 167, 169, 170

Epicure / 173
Eutopia Mixture / 171
Fashion / 158
Fast Mail / 168
Fountain / 173
Fragrant Mixture / 172
Game / 156
Geo. Washington / 158, 161, 162, 172
Gold Bond / 164
Golden Twins / 203
Golden Sceptre / 167
Gold Shore / 171, 175
Goodbodys / 173
Green Seal / 167
Half & Half / 164, 203
Hand Bag / 158
Hand Made / 163
Hi-Plane / 163
H-O / 160
Honest Labor / 168
Honest Weight / 175
Hurley Burley / 162
Just Suits / 158, 162, 172
Kentucky Club / 163
Kim-Bo / 164
Lafayette / 167
Lone Jack / 174
Long Distance / 161
Lord Salisbury / 174
Lucky Strike / 166, 174
Madeira / 166
Magnet / 161
Mail Pouch / 168, 175
Maryland Club / 168
Mastiff / 175
Mayo's / 160, 161
Monti Cristo / 169
Natural Leaf / 164
Navy / 160
Nigger Hair / 161
North Star / 169
Old Briar / 173
Old Colony / 163
Old English / 164
Oriental Mixture / 169

Osterloh's / 162
Our Advertiser / 175
Pat Hand / 169
Patterson / 159, 171
Pedro / 158, 161
Penny Post / 159
Philadelphia Mixture / 165
Philip Morris / 174
Piper Heidsieck / 164
Players Navy Cut / 166
Pride Of Virginia / 166
Prince Albert / 162
Puritan / 170
Q Boid / 163
Red J / 171
Regimental / 165
Richmond Club / 167
Round Trip / 171
Royal Worcester / 167
Seal of North Carolina / 162
Sensation / 159
Shot / 164
Sir Walter Raleigh / 170
Spurr's Best / 166
Stag / 164
Sterling / 175
Stripped / 156
Superior / 168
Sweet Burley / 172, 173
Sweet Cuba / 156, 158
Sweet Mist / 156
Three States / 169
Tiger / 157
Tuxedo / 162, 163
Twin Oaks / 166, 171
Union Commander / 159
Union Leader / 158, 161, 171, 172, 175, 203
U. S. Marine / 159
Van Bibber / 167
Velvet / 162, 164, 170, 203
Walnut / 165
Warnick & Brown / 159
Wild Fruit / 159, 172
Winner / 158, 160
Yoc-O-May / 166